Written with a blend o
Christie Somes' book i
children. She weaves together a personal story of her sexual violation as a child, illustrating exactly how child sexual assault happens, the journey of healing and most importantly, prevention. She delivers a profound message: It is not your fault, and you can heal! The courage demonstrated in these pages is heartwarming and important.

—Feather Berkower, LCSW Child Sexual Assault Prevention Educator & Author

I'm honored to recommend *Meet Carey Jones,* as a vital book to read for any adult survivor of child sexual abuse, as well as any parent or person committed to keeping children safe from this widespread harm. I stand in awe of Christie Somes' courage, brilliance, strength and heart, in addressing her own trauma, while learning about it so extensively and sharing that knowledge to guide and empower others. As a professional in the field of trauma recovery, I found Christie's explanations of trauma and healing to be clear, instructive and comprehensive. As a survivor of childhood sexual abuse, I was deeply moved by Christie's vulnerability in sharing her personal efforts to *Meet Carey Jones.* It gave me new insights into my own healing journey, for which I am grateful. As someone who knows we all must be aware of the realities of childhood sexual abuse in order to prevent, identify and treat this trauma as early as possible should it happen to children, I found ample resources to be more informed and aware through Christie's writing. This is an important book and a must read for all adults.

—Jennifer Stith, Executive Director, WINGS Foundation, Inc.

Christie Somes *with* Gerald D. Alpern, Ph.D.

# Meet Carey Jones

*Healing and Support for Survivors of Childhood Sexual Abuse and Practical Help for Parents and Educators*

Copyright © 2020 Christie Somes with Gerald D. Alpern, Ph.D.

All rights reserved. No part of this book may be used or reproduced by any means, graphic, electronic, or mechanical, including photocopying, recording, taping or by any information storage retrieval system without the written permission of the author except in the case of brief quotations embodied in critical articles and reviews.

This book is a work of non-fiction. Unless otherwise noted, the author and the publisher make no explicit guarantees as to the accuracy of the information contained in this book and in some cases, names of people and places have been altered to protect their privacy.

Archway Publishing books may be ordered through booksellers or by contacting:

Archway Publishing
1663 Liberty Drive
Bloomington, IN 47403
www.archwaypublishing.com
1 (888) 242-5904

Because of the dynamic nature of the Internet, any web addresses or links contained in this book may have changed since publication and may no longer be valid. The views expressed in this work are solely those of the author and do not necessarily reflect the views of the publisher, and the publisher hereby disclaims any responsibility for them.

Any people depicted in stock imagery provided by Getty Images are models, and such images are being used for illustrative purposes only. Certain stock imagery © Getty Images.

Author Photo by Paul Abdoo
CoAuthor Photo by Carol Alpern

Scripture quotations are taken from the Holy Bible, New Living Translation, copyright ©1996, 2004, 2015 by Tyndale House Foundation. Used by permission of Tyndale House Publishers, Inc., Carol Stream, Illinois 60188. All rights reserved.

ISBN: 978-1-4808-8751-0 (sc)
ISBN: 978-1-4808-8752-7 (hc)
ISBN: 978-1-4808-8753-4 (e)

Library of Congress Control Number: 2020907378

Print information available on the last page.

Archway Publishing rev. date: 05/20/2020

*To my children and grandchildren: May you learn from others' experiences, insights, and wisdom. May God always protect you and keep you safe from harm.*

## *Warning and Disclaimer*[1]

This book contains general information about childhood sexual abuse as well as other traumas. It is one person's personal story, in addition to much reference material. This book is not intended to replace the services of a professional mental health counselor or to provide professional psychological services to you. You should seek personal services if you need professional help.

Although the goal has been to make this book as accurate as possible, only current information up to the date of publication is possible. This book is simply meant to be one source of information regarding childhood sexual abuse. There is much information available and many sources can be used together to support individual needs.

# Contents

Foreword ........................................................... xi
Acknowledgments ........................................... xvii
Introduction .................................................. xxiii

## Part I: *A Well-Hidden Secret*

*Chapter 1*   A Well-Hidden Secret ................................. 3
*Chapter 2*   Therapy: The Process of Getting Help ......... 11
*Chapter 3*   A Visit with My Four-Year-Old Self ............. 22

## Part II: *Facts about Childhood Sexual Abuse*

*Chapter 4*   Facts and Myths about Childhood Sexual Abuse ........................................................ 37
*Chapter 5*   How Does Childhood Sexual Abuse Happen? ................................................................. 45

## Part III: *For Survivors*

*Chapter 6*   Adult Survivors of Childhood Sexual Abuse . 61
*Chapter 7*   Ego Defenses, Coping Strategies, and Muting the Pain ............................................................ 71

*Chapter 8*   Trauma and Posttraumatic Stress .................88
*Chapter 9*   Breaking the Silence ......................................99
*Chapter 10*  Triggers and Flashbacks ........................... 108
*Chapter 11*  Self-Care ................................................... 120
*Chapter 12*  Therapy and Support Groups .................... 129

## Part IV: *Practical Suggestions for Parents, Caregivers, and Educators*

*Chapter 13*  For Parents, Educators, and Caregivers ...... 141
*Chapter 14*  What To Do If Your Child Discloses They Have Been Sexually Abused ...................... 169
*Chapter 15*  Moving Forward ........................................ 178

*Appendix 1*  Organizations That Teach Prevention Programs for Adults and/or Children ......... 187
*Appendix 2*  Lorna Littner's List of Needs, Concerns, Learning Capabilities, Curiosities, and Behaviors .................................................. 189
*Appendix 3*  A Developmental Profile by Dr. Gerald D. Alpern ....................................................... 193

Age-Appropriate Book Recommendations ....................195
Bibliography ................................................................ 201
Endnotes ..................................................................... 203
About the Authors ........................................................211

# *Foreword*

Christie Somes is the ideal person to write this book. She knows what it is like to be sexually abused as a child. She knows what it is to suffer painful adult symptoms caused by childhood sexual abuse. She knows what it takes to seek, find, and utilize individual and group treatments for the abuse. And, finally, she has the courage, passion, and compassion to produce a very meaningful and useful book detailing her personal experiences.

*Meet Carey Jones* provides the most recent research and conclusions concerning multiple aspects of childhood sexual abuse. It is a book designed to aid others to combat the occurrence of childhood sexual abuse and help them find treatment.

When Christie, my former patient, told me of her decision to write this book, I volunteered to help in any way I could. I knew her to be a very bright and very caring person. I knew of her long and complex journey to render her unconscious conscious. I am pleased to have been invited to participate in this important work.

Childhood sexual abuse is a subject society has shied away from, yet the discussion is critical to the well-being of children as well as adults. This book focuses attention on childhood sexual abuse, its effects, how it occurs, and how it can be prevented and treated.

Cultural beliefs as well as scientific beliefs about the frequency, effects, and treatment of childhood sexual abuse have vacillated significantly over the past hundred years and continue to do so. Sigmund Freud, in the late 1800s, began the modern focus and confusion about childhood sexuality. Initially, he was surprised at the number of his patients who talked about sexual encounters with family members. More than once, he revised his theories about whether such accounts were accurate or fantasies and how either affected adult neuroses.

Moving forward to the second half of the twentieth century, psychotherapists believed early sexual abuse was the cause of many of their patients' problems. Subsequently, they encouraged legally confronting their accused abusers as part of their recovery. That was followed by a time when, again, the pendulum swung to thinking that many accounts of early (mostly family) abuse were not true. The strength of this latter belief was so strong as to generate a multitude of litigations against therapists for "creating false memories."

Currently, the debates continue. In recent years, psychiatric literature has proposed "the neurobiology of trauma." This concept purports that when sexual abuse occurs, there are physiological (hormonal) changes that lead to a collection of behavioral reactions such as freezing, not resisting advances, and, most importantly, rendering their memory about the event as inconsistent. These spotty memory effects offer a plausible explanation as to why so many of the descriptions of abusive sexual events tend to change over time.

The latest cultural direction is to strongly support adult victims of all kinds of sexual abuse. Such support is designed to free victims to report and seek help without being revictimized through accusations of inventing, inviting, or lying about the abuse because of changing descriptions of exactly what happened. Because the neurobiological explanation of the effects of trauma provides scientific reasons for inconsistencies in reporting abuse, many political and legal entities now accept reports of sexual abuse even when the description involves various inconsistencies. The recent #MeToo movement endorses the neurobiology of trauma and addresses a number of post-abuse problems such as why the descriptions tend to change with time, why the abuse may not be reported for years, and how the unwanted sexual actions could have occurred in the first place.

Continuing the disagreements about abuse, Richard McNally's 2003 book, *Remembering Trauma*, challenges this popular neurobiological description of trauma. His claim is that trauma does not lead to memory loss; in fact, it enhances memory for the trauma. As an example, he cites combat soldiers suffering from posttraumatic stress (PTS). There, he points out, the trauma is not forgotten at all. In fact, it is a hallmark of PTS that sufferers keep reliving well-remembered horrors of war.

Similarly, Susan Clancy in her 2010 book, *The Trauma Myth*, also disputes the biological theory, but she has a different criticism. She attempts to demonstrate the biological theory to be in error in its description of when the event actually causes the resulting trauma. Neither of these authors challenges the devastating effects of sexual abuse, but rather the way these traumas affect victims, which in turn, has major implications for how they can best be helped.

And so the debates about frequency, effects, and treatment continue.

The important takeaways from the history of the varying views about aspects of childhood sexual abuse are the following universally agreed upon basic conclusions:

1. Sexual abuse of children is not rare or uncommon.
2. Sexual activities with children are always wrong because they promote lifelong psychological damage to the personality.
3. The personality damage caused by childhood sexual abuse varies considerably between individuals.
4. Because the abuse takes so many different forms and produces so many different symptoms, no single treatment method can be expected to be universally effective for recovery or healing.
5. Enough is known about the ways sexual abuse occurs to provide useful guidelines for preventing and/or recognizing children's behaviors that are indicative of the threat or reality of sexual abuse.

The five conclusions above have been used to form the basis for this book:

First, the book aims at focusing attention on the possibility of the occurrence of childhood sexual abuse.

Second, it describes and explains the long-lasting significance of the damaging effects of such abuse.

Third, it reviews the wide range of psychological

handicaps that are commonly experienced during both childhood and adulthood as a result of early sexual abuse.

Fourth, it presents an informative overview of the most common therapeutic strategies currently used to combat the negative effects of childhood sexual abuse.

Fifth, the book's final chapters offer guidelines and specific suggestions for parents, teachers, and all caring adults for how to protect children from trauma, how to recognize trauma when it has occurred, and how to mitigate the debilitating effects of trauma when it does occur.

—Gerald D. Alpern, Ph.D.

# *Acknowledgments*

This book could not be a reality without the help, support, and encouragement from so many people.

This journey started with my therapist, Dr. Gerald D. Alpern, when I found the courage to tell, for the first time, what had happened to me when I was a small child. With his support and perseverance, we dealt with the subject of childhood sexual abuse and how it affected me for more than fifty years. We explored this subject and all of the resulting emotions for twelve years. While also dealing with other issues that came up, Jerry never wavered in his willingness to help me gain innumerable insights into childhood sexual abuse. We worked hard, and he stood by me through the worst moments.

Throughout this book project, Jerry continued his gentle inquiry regarding my progress, and he made himself openly available for ideas and counsel. Not only was his input important, but he also added the element of expertise. As the project grew, Jerry's input of knowledge, wisdom, editing, and writing increased, and I asked him if he would consider coauthoring this book.

Jerry's help with this book and my life, in general, has

been truly immeasurable. Jerry's countless hats remain filled, despite his retirement. Forever, I am grateful.

Along with Jerry's encouragement, he introduced me to Steve Alldredge of Steve Stories, who is accomplished in the field of writing and journalism. After our initial introduction, Steve encouraged me to go forward with this project because of our shared belief that the information might benefit even one person.

Steve helped me begin the process by asking me to write down my story and the struggles I encountered. Because of his expertise, we were able to organize this book into chapters that made sense. Steve helped with infinite research, and as a constant author advisor and editor, he played a key role in this project. Without Steve's help, this book would not exist.

Steve and I went to workshops, listened to speakers, read many books, blogs, and other literary sites, and spent countless hours on research. I give my many thanks to him for helping me bring *Meet Carey Jones* to life.

Most notably, Steve became dedicated to this project on an emotional level, and I have seen, firsthand, that he is a champion for sexual abuse survivors. Steve joined me in my quest to make a difference, and I am now pleased to call him my friend.

Dr. Jerry Alpern also introduced Lorna Littner, LMSW, a New York-based human sexuality educator, to me. Lorna's immense knowledge and expertise on the subject of sex education and appropriate behavior—as well as her insights into education regarding childhood sexual abuse—have proven to be abounding information and support for this project.

Lorna, too, added expertise to *Meet Carey Jones*. Moreover, knowing her enhances my life.

Jenny Stith, from WINGS Foundation in Denver, Colorado, has provided much information and a voice for those who have suffered from sexual abuse. She offered an abundance of knowledge, resources, and insights, while never failing to be a supportive, healing voice for all sexual abuse survivors.

Meghan Hurley Backofen, LCSW, from River Bridge Resource Center in Glenwood Springs, Colorado, was a valuable resource with her knowledge and experience of working with sexually abused children and their families. I have appreciated her warmth, encouragement, and plethora of information.

We were also fortunate to be embraced by many other professionals who were knowledgeable and experienced regarding the subject of childhood sexual abuse. I have been overwhelmed by the support of friends and, also, by the overwhelming support of professionals. Feather Berkower, LCSW and founder of Parenting Safe Children in Denver, Colorado, is a heroine to many survivors of childhood sexual abuse, and to parents, educators, and all caregivers of children because of her insightful information on prevention. Marilyn Van Derbur, a survivor of incest and a former Miss America, offers hope and healing to survivors of childhood sexual abuse and works with prevention organizations nationwide.

Archway Publishing has proven to be valuable. I am grateful for Michelle H., Chris D., the entire editorial team, and the Archway Publishing staff who helped make this book possible. Their professional insights, positive and useful comments, inclusion of all aspects of the publishing process, organization, and multiple areas of expertise provided worthwhile guidance.

My beautiful niece, Amy Diederich, who is a prosecutor and has seen numerous heinous crimes come through the criminal judicial process, was a cheering voice reaching out to me during my writing process. She was also helpful with edits and explanations that were confirming, astounding, and empowering.

Amy and my brother-in-law, Dan Somes, chief of police in Lindale, Texas, both spoke of vitally important childhood sexual abuse issues, processes, and protocols.

Karin Barker—one of the most well-read, kind, and intelligent people I know—has been an encouraging supporter, and her knowledge and edits were available at a moment's notice.

My husband, Scott, has been an undying supporter for me. He read every word, including every difficult passage, patiently listened to every thought, offered constructive input and comments, was constantly protective, and always knew how important this project is to me.

I remember telling Scott, for the first time, about my repeated sexual abuse incidents, and I remember his tears of sadness for what I had experienced, and his anger when he heard about the numerous assaults.

Scott has been a conscientious student in learning about the different types of sexual abuse, the different aspects of the issue, and the many long-term consequences.

Our children, Courtney, Coulter, Lynnie, and their spouses have lived through the many consequences of what happened to me without knowing any specifics. When I did finally disclose to them what happened, they offered love, support, and encouragement. They, too, were tearful, protective, and angry for what I had endured. They are all lights in my heart, and I love them dearly.

My sister and brother-in-law, Lynnie and Chris Tolk, and my brother, Jay, have loved and supported me in numerous, loving ways, and I am thankful for their love and prayers. In addition, there were several times that Lynnie and Chris allowed me to set up an office in their home during the writing of this book.

And then, there's my mom, who raised me and loved me and for whom some of the information in this book causes much pain. For that, I am truly sorry.

Mom, through this process, I have learned that not telling, being ashamed, and feeling bad are not uncommon among other sexual abuse survivors. You did nothing except love, support, and nourish me, always, and you continue to do so.

And, finally, I offer my many thanks to Carey Jones, my imaginary friend. With all of her complexities, Carey represents everything good. She is a combination of all of the meaningful people in my life. She loved me, while knowing about everything that was happening to me that was bad. In the book, I referenced this to perhaps a child feeling God's presence, which is the closest concept I am able to describe. I am blessed to have had Carey Jones as my friend, and I am blessed to be a child of God.

# *Introduction*

> *A central point needs to be highlighted again: Sexual abuse is damaging no matter how the victim's body is violated. At first, many will doubt the veracity of that claim. But in every case of abuse, the dignity and beauty of the soul have been violated.*
> —Dan Allender, psychologist and author of *The Wounded Heart: Hope for Adult Victims of Childhood Sexual Abuse*

It took many years of my life and much therapy to accept and admit how the sexual abuse I endured when I was four and five years old has significantly impacted me on a regular basis for more than fifty years.

Including my personal story in this book is an attempt to openly describe my process in order to alert and educate others about the signs, symptoms, defenses, and treatment of childhood sexual abuse and how it affects you. Hopefully, my stumbles throughout the healing process can help others effectively be in touch with emotions that they might be feeling but haven't been able to articulate or maybe even admit to themselves.

Through individual and support group therapies, I have learned that trauma has many debilitating effects, and it wreaks havoc at unexpected times as the unconscious mind attempts to protect us by burying negative memories.

A major reason for this book's existence is the hope that dispelling false assumptions can prevent others from suffering lifelong emotional damage because of a childhood event.

Two very commonly held false beliefs were the roots of why I didn't address the significant effects of my personal experience of being sexually abused as a child.

I experienced the first set of false beliefs as a young child. I thought that what happened to me was because I was a bad girl or that being abused turned me into a bad girl. At that time, I didn't know the concept of sexual abuse. I was ashamed of what happened and worried that I would be blamed, so I never told anyone. Those childhood beliefs are so common among children that child caregivers, such as parents and teachers, need to actively counter the possibility of such ideas with children very early in their lives.

I experienced the second set of false beliefs as an adult. These beliefs were not—and are not—unique to me. Many adults hold these same feelings as well. It involves thinking that only genital contact or some form of intercourse is what defines sexual abuse, which is not true. In fact, long-term, devastating personality effects can result from much less physically intrusive behaviors.

## What Is Childhood Sexual Abuse?

The World Health Organization defines childhood sexual abuse (CSA) as:

> The involvement of a child in sexual activity that he or she does not fully comprehend, is unable to give informed consent to, or for which the child is not developmentally prepared, or else that violates the laws or social taboos of society. Children can be sexually abused by both adults and other children who are—by virtue of their age or stage of development—in a position of responsibility, trust, or power over the victim.[2]

Child sexual abuse can include physical and nonphysical contact between a perpetrator and a child. Both verbal and visual abuse can also be identified as sexual abuse. Some forms of physical child sexual abuse include fondling; intercourse; masturbation in the presence of a minor or forcing the minor to masturbate; sex of any kind with a minor, including vaginal, oral, or anal; sex trafficking; or any other sexual conduct that is harmful to a child's mental, emotional, or physical welfare.

Legal definitions of sexual abuse vary widely from state to state, as does the age of consent. There are a number of factors that determine if a person legally consents, from their age to whether they're incapacitated.

Although the WHO definition is comprehensive, local legal action is based on the legal definition of sexual abuse in your state and is often based on the age or ages of the children involved and the state's age of consent.

## How Therapy Helped Me

The process of therapy uncovered the fact that I was hiding from a multitude of effects of my childhood sexual abuse.

In therapy, I learned I had to face the resurrection of a past I thought had been put to rest. That's when I began my personal journey of recovery, and I learned that seemingly unrelated adverse childhood experiences (ACEs) were, in fact, interrelated and relevant to my life.

I know how much my experience of childhood sexual abuse has profoundly affected my life. I also know others who have endured very different forms of sexual, traumatic experiences, yet also suffer from adult problems very similar to my own. The commonality between my story and theirs is the lasting impact the abuse has had on our lives, even though the abuse was completely different in form and situation. I now know that sexual abuse cannot be simply classified as severe, moderate, or mild on the basis of what form it took. I now know that devastating impacts can come from sexual behavior ranging from forced rape to verbal abuse.

## Prevention

Parents and educators need to be aware of and be able to recognize subtle clues or behaviors in children that might lead to better-crafted discussions or interventions.

Most parents have told their children that they can tell them anything without fear of punishing consequences. However, it takes special and often-repeated discussions and behaviors to convince children to trust anyone, including parents, when embarrassment or guilt feelings are involved, especially when perpetrators are masters at manipulating children. Children often try to protect parents and siblings from abusers by not telling what happened to them.

Part IV includes the kinds of conversations and awareness to have with children and the importance of being a safe person in their lives. Although this information is focused on body-safety rules and sexual abuse prevention, it is applicable to numerous areas in life.

With equal importance, I seek to offer support to adult survivors of childhood sexual abuse. Most of all, I want them to believe that healing can begin at any age.

It is paramount that all survivors of sexual abuse accept that healing is not a linear voyage. Triggers can be expected to cause setbacks. But being able to navigate through setbacks is an important step in growth and healing. I, like most adults dealing with sexual abuse, experienced progress intermingled with occasional setbacks. However, those setbacks eventually proved to be a valuable part of the healing process as I learned about triggers, why they occur, and what can be learned from them. Re-traumatizing is often part of the process. You have to go through it.

In part I of the book, I briefly use my story to highlight how childhood sexual abuse affected me and how I was helped with therapy and support groups. In part II, I discuss the issue of childhood sexual abuse, including facts, signs of abuse, and possible long-term effects. In part III, I detail many of the common effects survivors of childhood sexual abuse experience, noting that each individual's story is different. And in part IV, with the help of professionals, I discuss methods for parents, educators, and others to have open communication and trusting relationships with children that encourage them to talk with you without hesitation when something inappropriate happens.

Well into the journey of writing *Meet Carey Jones*, unexpected worldwide outrage against sexual harassment and abuse shot to the forefront of international news with the #MeToo campaign affecting Hollywood, the media, sports organizations, universities, and many different business industries. The #MeToo movement has hit a collective, palpable nerve, and many atrocious stories have come to light and been told. The heightened awareness and open exchanges are creating an important change in acceptable behavior and education, prompting fundamental changes in how businesses, schools, sports organizations, and individuals operate.

In the past, the subjects of sexual harassment and childhood sexual abuse have been deeply uncomfortable for most people to discuss. Joyce Marter is a therapist and the founder of Urban Balance, a company that provides premier psychotherapy services for individuals, couples, families, adolescents, and children. She said, "There's normalization and validation in this movement as it takes away the shame, secrecy, and stigma that is so common in situations of abuse."[3]

After the launch of #MeToo, I encountered a resurgence of an old familiar thought: that the form of sexual abuse I experienced was insignificant. Rather than feeling empowered, I felt shame about having the audacity to compare my abuse to others' abuse. Ultimately, I was successful in realizing and acknowledging the deep-rooted shame that had resurfaced, and I was able to work through this setback.

The regression served as a valuable, gentle lesson about many myths and misconceptions of what survivors of childhood sexual abuse experience—and the many reasons so many survivors' voices are silenced before they ever tell anyone what happened to them.

Through research, helpful information was unearthed from therapeutic professionals, books, articles, websites, and personal stories to create *Meet Carey Jones*. This collected information helps illustrate the shared difficulty in confronting the issue of sexual abuse and explaining the internalized shame that can appear in so many different areas of life.

I would tell all victims and survivors of sexual assault or any abuse that self-compassion is an ongoing quest. You are stronger than you think, and, if you have been sexually abused, dealing with the authentic truth will make you stronger for yourself and for your loved ones.

The process of healing from sexual abuse is difficult, but ultimately, it is a fulfilling journey. For me, there were aspects that led to unexpected, challenging, rewarding, uplifting, transforming, effective, and extraordinary growth. In fact, the process and being open to the raw emotion of my therapeutic journey proved useful to me in many aspects of my life.

My hopes and desires are to somehow shorten or ease others' battles with the aftereffects and consequences of childhood sexual abuse. Insights learned through my story, coupled with information from experts, will lead to effective techniques for recovery and the prevention of future sexual abuse of children.

—Christie Somes
Fall 2019

# Part I

*A Well-Hidden Secret*

## Chapter 1

# A Well-Hidden Secret

*Before we can heal and let go, what ails us deeply must first come to the surface.*

—Anonymous

## Meet Carey Jones

Carey Jones was my imaginary friend, my major companion, and my only confidante when I was four and five years old. I cherished her because she knew and understood everything about me without having to tell her anything, and she loved me anyway. She gave me compassion, comfort, understanding, and nonjudgmental support.

I don't remember the details of creating Carey Jones. Physically, I just felt her presence; I never needed to create an image of her. It was enough to know her essence. She was always there for me, and she intuitively knew my hidden thoughts and emotions.

In my mind, Carey represented everything that is good—everything anyone would want in a friend.

As I grew older, it became common knowledge within our family that I had created an imaginary friend when I was young. Every Christmas, I received a gift from Carey Jones, which was my mother's loving gesture. At one point, when I was older, I asked my mother how she knew that Carey Jones was my imaginary friend. With a warm smile, my mother gently explained that it wasn't hard to discern after walking into a room where I was having a conversation at a tea party, but I was the only person in the room.

I remember feeling that Carey was truly there. I remember the table and setting the many tea parties for two people. In my heart, I had a simple inner knowing of a greater presence accompanying me. Now, with my belief system and faith, I would say that Carey Jones was my young child's version of feeling God's presence—or my guardian angel.

## Therapy: A Life-Changing Process

I started seeing my therapist, Dr. Gerald D. Alpern (I will refer to him as Jerry throughout this book because that was his preference during our therapy process), when I was forty-four years old. I was in deep emotional pain about some life experiences that were troubling me. I had always believed that seeking therapy was a sign of strength, never weakness. It was a particularly stressful time of my life, and I heeded my own advice.

Not quite a year after I began therapy, I was in the

confines of my therapist's office when he asked a question about my early childhood.

I paused—actually, I froze—as I considered whether or not to reveal what I had kept from everyone or blatantly lie to my trusted, nonjudgmental therapist.

I found the courage to tell Jerry the complete story:

> I was four, almost five years old, playing outside my house in my sandbox, when one of the older boys who lived in the neighborhood began to chase me. Of course, he caught me. He lifted my skirt, pulled down my underwear, forced me to bend over, and plunged a stick into my anus so violently that I bled. On many other days, this same boy repeated the same act with the same excruciating ending.

Jerry asked me if I had told anyone what had happened to me when I was a little girl, and my answer was no. Carey Jones was the only one who knew what had happened to me.

Why didn't I tell anyone? I didn't tell because in my four- and five-year-old mind, I felt ashamed, dirty, and bad. I thought if I told, I would be in trouble, and my parents would be angry and punish me.

What I did do to cover my "crime" was pull my clothes back on as best I could, get to a bathroom back at my home, and wash my panties and myself in an attempt to hide my secret shame. Then, for more than forty years, I did my best to forget my sexual assaults.

"That was sexual abuse, Christie," Jerry responded, and

there was a sudden silence in the room. Inside, I shook and shuddered, and my heart beat rapidly.

What had happened to me was something I had known for years, yet I was surprised and horrified, and I had a difficult time understanding that I had been sexually abused. I had never made that connection, always harboring the childhood belief that I had done something bad. I had never considered the situation as anything beyond my shame and guilt.

Hearing those words "sexual abuse" was significantly helpful, but it was also heavy. I had completely hidden from others what I considered a shameful secret. I had even buried much of it from myself.

I remember crying—weeping—when I heard Jerry acknowledge that he understood how I had come to believe and feel that I was a bad person. Over time, a major goal of therapy became learning that I was *not* at fault, I was *not* to blame, and I was *not* dirty and should *not* feel ashamed or unworthy of being protected. I was *not* guilty of anything. I had been a victim of sexual abuse that had been impossible for me to process as a four- and five-year-old child.

That therapy appointment was life changing, but understanding intellectually that I had been sexually abused was not the end of my journey. I was not instantly cured. In reality, it was merely the beginning, and to this day, there continue to be definite periods of regression. It took a long, long time to genuinely accept and act on those insights into the feelings and thoughts that had influenced my self-concept and behaviors for so long.

Before therapy, if I thought about the attacks at all, it

was just as a dirty childhood secret that I wouldn't share with anyone—and it never occurred to me that the abuse had been sexual.

> *Tiptoe if you must, but take the first step.*
> —Naeem Calloway

## Intellectual and Emotional Insights

Going through the process of therapy, there are both intellectual and emotional insights. Although intellectual insight is important, emotional insight is more critical for one's psychological health. Having emotional insight and understanding means you feel it in the gut, which is more powerful than a belief in your mind. Sometimes, you might respond emotionally to a situation while not having any awareness about or insight into why such a response is occurring.

Intellectual insight happens when you are able to consciously address and grasp an idea. An example would be a man who can't hold a job because he gets into fights with his bosses. The man subconsciously compares each boss to his dictatorial, unreasonable father. When his therapist points out this connection, the man understands.

Emotional insight happens when you can embrace and truly understand a concept at the feeling level. It is much easier to act on something when you understand it at the emotional level than when you solely understand it intellectually. An emotional insight using the same example as above would have the man understand the connection on his own without anyone pointing it out to him, realizing that his boss is being reasonable and is really not like his father.

Many times, I felt overwhelmed and in turmoil as I uncovered the roots of many of my negative self-beliefs and behaviors.

I know now that both the FBI and the Department of Justice define rape as "penetration no matter how slight, of the vagina or anus with any body part or object, or oral penetration by a sex organ of another person, without the consent of the victim."[4]

I now understand that I was anally raped on a number of occasions over a period of time. But even when the abuse does not involve rape by its legal definition, it can cause significant psychological and emotional damage.

Therapy provided me a slow progression that required much internal digging to allow me to develop a new way of thinking and feeling and to consciously think for myself.

As part of my learning and healing process, I have realized that the thing I most regret is not telling my mother about what was happening to me. Realizing as a middle-aged adult that I would have benefited from telling my parents that the neighbor boy was regularly hurting me has caused both pain and relief simultaneously.

Hearing my story brings tears to my mom's eyes to this day. *Now*, I know that she would have protected me, nurtured me, and made sure that this would never happen to me again. But as a little four- and five-year-old girl, I didn't know any of this, which created serious consequences that I suffered as an adult.

I feel much sorrow that I did not tell my mother because

of the pain that I have caused. If I had told her, not only would the abuse have been stopped, but I also wouldn't have found myself in a situation later in life striving to heal many detrimental beliefs about myself that generated a collection of dysfunctional behaviors. I also regret not telling anyone because it haunts me wondering if my perpetrator ever harmed anyone else in any way or whether or not he was being abused himself.

This was especially astounding to me because when I told my story of abuse to Jerry, I was in the midst of lovingly raising three children with my husband. Without a doubt, I would protect them, love them, and support them. I knew that, but from the time I was a small child until I was a middle-aged adult, I wasn't able to accept that I had been worthy of that same protection—even though I had been raised in a loving home. I had kept this secret to myself for so long, and as a result, I had not allowed anyone to help me. I now know this is a common experience of many who have been sexually abused.

In *Miss America by Day,* former Miss America Marilyn Van Derbur writes, "Most children don't tell. Most adults don't tell. It's usually because of overwhelming shame. Many survivors carry their secrets for decades."[5]

As mentioned in the introduction, perhaps a new era of childhood education, adult education, and release of shame will be a positive outcome as a result of recent cultural developments and the #MeToo movement.

Returning to the opening quote of this chapter, before I could begin to "heal and let go," I first had to let my secret "come to the surface."

I have lived the terrible consequences of keeping my abuse secret and not acknowledging the real effects of that abuse until decades after it happened. At the same time, I'm on a healing journey. By talking with a qualified professional who guides me, I have learned that I am not alone in how I have suffered.

## Chapter 2

# Therapy: The Process of Getting Help

> *Courage doesn't happen when you have all the answers. It happens when you are ready to face the questions you have been avoiding your whole life.*
>
> —Shannon L. Alder

Overcoming trauma can be transformative. Fortunately, I have been on a healing path with the help of psychotherapy.

When I was young, remembering details of my assaults and bringing the memories to consciousness just brought shame. Instead, I conveniently shoved those experiences into a hidden place, and I didn't deal with them. But the shame didn't go away, and I suffered from behaviors that compromised the quality of my life.

Even though I had a supportive, loving family, I can remember feelings of self-doubt and unworthiness that were forever present in my life from early childhood. I never understood the root of them—and I never aimed to understand them—until I began therapy years later. It took therapy to understand my earlier childhood traumas and their effects on my self-concept.

Understanding that painful self-concept has been a long, hard journey of progress, temporary setbacks, and then more growth.

Gratefully, I have more awareness now, and I am better equipped to rationally deal with issues of self-doubt when they arise. I have been successful at greatly mitigating my early beliefs about myself, and those unwanted feelings are now much less of a factor in my life. For years, I was thoroughly unaware of any relationship between my self-beliefs, negative self-talk, self-worth, and what had happened to me when I was four and five years old.

Up to that point, I had lived much of my life in denial, secrecy, and unawareness. That being said, I enjoyed my life. In spite of a diminished self-concept, I had meaningful friendships, a wonderful marriage, and three incredible children. I had a genuine appreciation for life, but I carried a secret that brought much internal shame, unconscious thoughts, and unconscious behaviors. It was a secret that prevented me from being totally authentic because I felt shame and never considered revealing that part of myself.

Taking the step and making the commitment to seek therapy takes courage and strength. It's a difficult challenge to admit that help is needed. It's also a challenge to have the backbone to seek help, especially if others close to you might not understand or support the decision. Gratefully, my family was supportive of my choice to be in therapy.

## Finding a Therapist

Therapy can be an instrumental and valuable tool in healing, but not all therapies or therapists are of equal value. You need to carefully evaluate to find a therapy process that can work for you.

The decision to begin therapy can bring much anxiety. I remember wondering if I could ever explain anything well enough or articulate my feelings successfully. It felt overwhelming.

I strongly believe that the first necessity for therapy is finding a therapist with whom you can form a therapeutic alliance. Therapeutic alliance refers to a client and their chosen therapist working as a team—while sharing goals and methods for reaching those goals. Most critically, the parties trust each other and work well together.

According to my therapist, Jerry, the quality of the therapeutic alliance is a strong predictor for the quality of the outcome of therapy. Practically, this means that when someone begins a treatment course, they should share a genuine bond while they are in treatment; if they do not, they should seek help elsewhere.

Forging a good therapeutic alliance takes time. It is recommended that there be a minimum of two or three contacts before making that decision because frequently during the course of treatment, there can be ruptures in the alliance. Research shows that ruptures that are repaired lead to better outcomes than alliances without any ruptures. Like successful marriages, being able to survive periods of alienation, whatever the cause, strengthens the relationship.

Jerry and I developed a strong therapeutic alliance, and

after having experienced that strong alliance with him, I cannot imagine therapy working any other way. We shared a mutual respect for one another, which blossomed and grew, and our strong alliance helped me explore my thoughts and find insights.

Personally, the characteristics that proved to be essential and nonnegotiable in my therapy were trust, empathy, and warmth. Jerry was genuinely interested in helping me, and he was patient and able to communicate in a way that I understood when I was blocked. Essentially, Jerry encouraged me to be as authentic and transparent as I could possibly be, and we adapted our approach or the topic depending on what life presented. He never failed to point out his own beliefs, while being sensitive, honoring my belief system, demonstrating self-insight, and being dependably there for me.

Over time, Jerry and I were very flexible with our therapy appointments. During the process, we tried different forms of therapy that have proven useful for others. Some of them worked for me, and some of them didn't.

The course of therapy can vary widely depending on personal circumstances. Some people successfully conclude therapy following a few sessions; others seek therapy or groups for years or require lifelong support.

My therapy with Jerry was over the course of twelve years. At times, I went to therapy appointments once per week; other times, it was once every few weeks, once per month, or every six weeks, and I mixed this combination with a few hiatus periods, which could last for up to four months. Sometimes my hiatus breaks were planned; at other times, we learned that they were part of my resistance during an especially challenging time or subject. Ultimately, the resistance was invariably instructive.

> *I'm fine. Well, I'm not fine—I'm here. Is there something wrong with that? Absolutely.*
> —Ned Vizzini, *It's Kind of a Funny Story*

## Resistance to Therapy

As Sigmund Freud stated, "Therapy is really the slow destruction of resistance." There were many times when I was completely unaware of being resistant, even if it was brought to my attention. Ironically, this characteristic fits right in the Wikipedia definition of resistance:

> Resistance refers to oppositional behavior when an individual's unconscious defenses of the ego are threatened by an external source. This would be for the purpose of inhibiting the revelation of any repressed information from within the unconscious mind.

I learned that I could be resistant to all kinds of insights. I learned that the brain is intuitively protective and consciously only lets in information about painful experiences one is ready to face. The memories get literally shoved to the unconscious part of the brain and become secrets we keep from ourselves. However, I found that it was well worth the effort to keep working to peel back the layers.

Each person responds to situations differently and in their own time frame. Finding the balance of facing resistance and uncovering the painful experiences, while being patient when the topic submerges deep below the surface, is a stressful task worth all of the ultimate rewards of insight. However, at the time, this didn't always seem true.

Resistance could consist of deciding there was no time for therapy altogether or canceling scheduled appointments. Resistance could be my refusal to talk about an emotional topic at hand, either consciously or unconsciously. Even though it was wearisome, I am grateful that my therapist gently prodded me to stay on task, while backing off when necessary, as I experienced a mixture of feelings: relief, anger, sadness, gratitude, fear, or calm.

Sometimes during a setback, you can feel as though any progress made up to that point is irrelevant. Although periods of regression continued occasionally during therapy, they happened less frequently, and for a shorter duration. When they did occur, I rationally and intellectually knew that I was not back at square one, even though it often felt that way.

At times during my voyage, there were painful topics that produced severe anxiety and absolute muteness. Through the difficult process of living through my own resistance, I eventually learned that facing the resistance is really where the self-growth happens. Without a doubt, it is difficult, and it can feel overwhelming. I found that the magic happens by really staying focused on the situation at hand, gnawing on it, and facing truths.

It's not really magic; it's hard work for both the therapist and the patient. Facing any resistance and breaking through it can be both exhausting and liberating. Commitment is crucial in this process, even through resistance, and it is especially vital to be committed during periods of resistance.

## Gaining Awareness

During therapy sessions, when heavy issues gained clarity, both intellectually and emotionally, it was an exhilarating and rewarding experience. Eventually, I learned that I had lived in denial from some truths because I subconsciously felt that acknowledgment would confirm and expose that I was bad. I feared that if others knew the real truth about me, their disgust with me would prove my self-beliefs. Subconsciously, my internal torment made me feel like a fraud.

Throughout therapy, I learned to observe my own behaviors. I elevated my awareness concerning various issues, and I discovered much about myself. In essence, by working with a therapist, I learned a better way of sometimes being my own therapist.

There were times when I dreaded an upcoming therapy appointment, and at other times, I looked forward to an appointment. I eventually learned that when I subconsciously discredited my own thoughts and opinions, these feelings were rooted in my abuse-generated feelings of unworthiness.

We discovered this would carry over in my general life, which meant that I routinely was submissive—even in friendships. I had learned submissiveness at an early age. Although I always tried to run away and avoid the situation of being abused by the neighborhood boy, I did not fight back or tell anyone, acts which could be viewed as submissive.

Now that I have more awareness, I have made much

progress. For quite some time, I didn't allow myself to candidly feel anything negative regarding Jerry. He helped me see that I was frequently unable to allow myself to acknowledge when I disagreed with or felt anger toward him. He also helped me recognize that any worthwhile relationship has ups and downs.

More recently, I can admit that I became angry or frustrated with Jerry on a number of occasions. It was a difficult and valuable lesson that led to being able to view my therapist more authentically, and I gained even more respect for him during that process. As a result, a richer level of insights occurred.

I remember a major conversation when I found the courage to tell Jerry that I thought he was being disingenuous, which turned into much grist for our therapy. This discussion occurred when he explained that he believed me to be a good and valuable person and that he deeply cared about my happiness. It took years to understand that my feelings that he was disingenuous had nothing to do with Jerry. Those thoughts had to do with how I was personally feeling at the time regarding my own self-worth. This was a profound aha moment.

> *The trees are about to show us how lovely*
> *it is to let the dead things go.*
> —Anonymous

## Painful Personal Issues

During the course of many years of therapy, many issues were discussed. Painstakingly, Jerry and I discovered that many of them were the direct result of what another person inflicted upon me when I was a child.

For me, there were two particular subjects that were extremely dark and painful. The first subject we called my "fall malaise," my severe, debilitating reaction to autumn for so many years.

Fall is a beautiful season. However, the experiences—the smells of autumn, the crunching leaves under my feet, that "fall feel in the air," the beginning of the school year, and my birthday—were filled with dread and anxiety, which I masked throughout my life because I didn't understand the reasons. For years, it was an entire season of paralysis, fear, and a powerful sense of unsettled hopelessness that could feel like impending doom. For me, fall can be a season of dissociation, self-sabotage, self-deprecation, and negative self-judgment.

It is amazing, but true, that many major insights seem so obvious once revealed and accepted. Over time, and after the result of much work to undo the churning debilitating fall syndrome, we painfully discovered my sexual abuse occurred during fall, and it was directly related to my feeling of the fall malaise.

I have learned that although I may occasionally lose my balance in fall with triggers that set me off, and put me right back on the path of self-deprecation and self-sabotage, I continue to work on embracing my immense progress with the compassion and knowledge that I am healthier as a result of deep personal work and God's grace.

At some point in our discovery, I remember discussing the second dark topic with Jerry, a topic that made me literally sick to my stomach and scared. I felt sure that nobody would be able to understand the depth of this issue with me—and that it was disgusting, unacceptable, painful, embarrassing, and humiliating.

I am an emotional eater, and I had always kept that fact extremely private. Even though I had become comfortable talking with Jerry about a wide array of topics, I was extremely uncomfortable talking with him about this issue. After much talk with Jerry, I eventually discovered some insight into my eating. He described just how profoundly my neuroses were linked—that being sick to my stomach and scared about giving details of my shameful eating were very much like the fact that I was too scared to tell my mother about my early childhood sexual abuse.

Jerry explained that the eating had become the psychological equivalent of that little girl's anal rapes, of which I/she was so very ashamed. Inappropriate eating was my neurotic way of recreating the shame I felt as a sexually abused child. I was recreating the shameful secret sexual events with shameful secret eating events, and I taught myself this behavior when I was a young child.

While it has taken considerable dedicated work to unblock memories that were buried for more than forty years, awareness is a liberating reward. Although painful at times, living mindfully has the healing potential of enhancing your life. Therapy takes patience and perseverance. Through the process of working through the challenges, the end result is real personal growth.

For me, my path to healing began with finding a therapist with whom I had a good working relationship. As a result of that therapy, I am on a healing path—and I continue to transform. I would never say that I am completely healed of the effects and behaviors of my early childhood abuse, but I would say that I now understand those behaviors and effects much more. Because of that understanding and the work with my therapist, I am often able to realize when those behaviors arise, and I am able to work through them.

> *"For I know the plans I have for you," says the Lord. "They are plans for good and not for disaster, to give you a future and a hope."*[6]
>
> —Jeremiah 29:11

## Chapter 3

# A Visit with My Four-Year-Old Self

*I'm going to make you so proud.*
—Note to self

*Promise me you'll always remember: You're braver than you believe and stronger than you seem, and smarter than you think.*
—Christopher Robin to Pooh in Disney's *Winnie the Pooh*

It's common knowledge that the events of childhood influence people throughout their lives. Sigmund Freud was the first of many psychologists to believe that many important events and conditioned beliefs reside in our unconscious, rather than conscious, mind.

We may well remember major chunks of our childhood, but humans tend to forget certain unpleasant things, especially when they feel responsible for them. It is the uncomfortable material delegated to our unconscious that has a profound influence on many critical aspects of our personality. For instance, our romantic inclinations for those with particular physical attributes or behaviors are often based on what we learned to appreciate, but no longer remember, from childhood.

The most critical beliefs and attitudes that were conditioned during childhood are those associated with our self-concepts. Personal judgments concerning our competency and our lovability are primarily laid down during childhood, and many of these—usually the negative ones—are only subconsciously remembered.

Because of the natural incompetence and dependence that defines childhood, all of us retain in our unconsciousness what psychologists have labeled our *inner insecure child*. This universal insecurity is exacerbated for those who suffer trauma, neglect, or abuse during childhood. For those children, their inner insecure child has a much larger impact on the quality of their lives. The most common unconscious damage from abuse is a negative self-concept. Sufferers may be aware of not liking themselves, but more often, the unconscious insecurities are expressed through depressions, anxieties, or feelings of being unworthy, incompetent, and/or unlovable.

Amazon lists more than 250 books regarding inner child work. Most of the work involves some form of re-parenting in order to remove the negative self-concepts formed prior to what one learned before puberty.

Sufferers from any of these painful conditions frequently seek out mental health professionals with the obvious goal of eradicating or at least minimizing such symptoms. There are a multitude of therapy approaches available to address the presenting problem of insecurities rooted in childhood.

In cases where the patient's symptoms are significantly related to an aspect of childhood, the therapy frequently takes some form of what has been labeled *inner child work*. Inner child work typically involves some form of re-parenting through a fantasized interaction between the compassionate, knowledgeable adult and the inner insecure child. This fantasized interaction can be done by the therapist serving as a surrogate parent and/or by the patient through specialized role-playing to relive childhood traumas in a therapeutic way. For example, one such fantasized interaction might have the patient remembering problematic childhood events and then injecting healthier interpretations into the consciousness to tell the child that the trauma was not their fault.

My therapist, Jerry, taught a combination of guided fantasies, with the work being done by having either the therapist or the patient construct and carry out the fantasized interaction.

The fantasized interaction is designed to comfort the child and—as directly as possible—alleviate the child's beliefs that underlie the symptoms. Once the traumatic events or erroneous belief system is made conscious, the symptom is available for intellectual and/or emotional insight.

For example, some therapy clients are self-punishing as adults for childhood actions they feel were their fault. They may not remember the action that generated the guilt, but the guilt drives their self-destructive adult behaviors. Once that guilt is worked through as being inappropriate, the motivation for adult self-imposed damaging can disappear (emotional insight) or be minimized through logically working through the behaviors (intellectual insight).

The re-parenting fantasy interaction begins with the adult working to remember details about themselves at the age the child needs to be visited and reprogrammed. What was their bedroom like then? What clothing did they wear? What friends or relatives did they interact with at that time? Once a sufficient memory of the to-be-visited child has been created, the fantasy of being with that child is started.

From there, it depends on what aspect of the insecure child is being addressed. It could be simply comforting the child. More often, it's convincing the child their beliefs about being unlovable, guilty, or inherently bad are untrue. It could also be reassuring the child of their inherent strengths by telling them of the future, such as, "You will have academic, social, romantic, monetary, or status successes." It might be by explaining to the child in terms that are understandable to their age and capacity that they were not to blame for whatever is causing guilt, depression, or anxiety.

The technique is successful when the end of the visit or visits impacts the adult's symptoms. Theoretically, what has happened is that the false beliefs from their childhood have been undermined so that the guilt or depression has been therapeutically impacted. It's very much like a medication that ends a medical symptom such as a headache or a stomach disorder. The symptom is gone with only minimal understanding of exactly how the pill did its job.

When successful, the adult may report that the experience produced healing, compassion, and love for the insecure inner child and always some form of relief. A typical response is the reporting of the individual just feeling more relaxed and sure.

Sometimes, offering the client intellectual understanding of what happened is useful, and it can even further the potency of the treatment. At other times, the client need not understand the mechanism of correcting the unconscious thinking error. Feeling symptom relief is all that was sought, and theoretical knowledge adds little importance.

Robert Burney is an author, spiritual teacher, codependence counselor, and grief therapist who has written about his research with inner child work:

> It is through having the courage and willingness to revisit the emotional dark night of the soul that was our childhood that we can start to understand on a gut level why we have lived our lives as we have.
>
> It is when we start understanding the cause and effect relationship between what happened to the child that we were, and the effect it had on the adult we became, that we can Truly start to forgive ourselves. It is only when we start understanding on an emotional level, on a gut level, that we were powerless to do anything any differently than we did that we can Truly start to Love ourselves.
>
> The hardest thing for any of us to do is to have compassion for ourselves. As children, we felt responsible for the things that happened to us. We blamed ourselves for the things that were done to us and for the deprivations we suffered. There is nothing more powerful in this transformational process than being able to go back to that child who still exists within us and say,

"It wasn't your fault. You didn't do anything wrong, you were just a little kid."[7]

And he continues:

> As long as we are judging and shaming ourselves we are giving power to the disease. We are feeding the monster that is devouring us.
>
> We need to take responsibility without taking the blame. We need to own and honor the feelings without being a victim of them.
>
> We need to rescue and nurture and Love our inner children—and STOP them from controlling our lives. STOP them from driving the bus! Children are not supposed to drive, they are not supposed to be in control.
>
> And they are not supposed to be abused and abandoned. We have been doing it backward. We abandoned and abused our inner children. Locked them in a dark place within us. And at the same time let the children drive the bus—let the children's wounds dictate our lives.[8]

## My Visit

Dealing with childhood sexual assault is a painful experience, and aspects of the healing process took me outside of my comfort zone. For example, I was uncomfortable when Jerry suggested that I "pay a visit" to my four-year-old self. When I first heard his suggestion, I was completely closed off to the idea. But later, driving home, I thought about his suggestion again because Jerry believed it could be useful.

Days later, without saying anything to Jerry, I decided to give the inner child work a try in the privacy of my own home. It was an exercise in a willingness to heal, a willingness to imagine, and a willingness to try something that seemed nonsensical. It was a powerful experience that I will never forget.

Given my initial resistance, I was surprised to find myself easily envisioning being with my little four-year-old self.

Actually, I found her outside in the sandbox, where I often played. In my scenario, I visualized that the present-day me got down in that sandbox with my four-year-old self, we took out all the shovels and the bucket, and we made a castle surrounded by a moat. Then, I started weeping.

The moat was for protection. We put water in the moat, and the sand in the sandbox turned to mud. She crawled up into my lap—just as I have held all three of my children thousands of times over the years to comfort them. This was all an imaginative journey, but it seemed real to me.

First, she buried her little head in my shoulder and neck and wept. I didn't have to tell her who I was, but she knew—just like Carey Jones knew what I was thinking without me having to say anything.

We cried and cried. And then we cried some more.

She asked me how old I was, and when I told her, she thought I was old! Her very next question was if we were bad. As we sat in that sandbox and talked, she nuzzled into me.

I was very conscious of wanting to tell her only what was appropriate for a four-year-old to hear. I didn't want her to know the scope of the struggle it has been for me to recover and heal or that I still sometimes feel like I am bad.

I took a deep breath. I told her we are good. I told her we like to have fun, but sometimes we think we don't deserve good or happy things, and I told her to try really hard not to believe that we're unworthy because it's a lie.

I told her that it's okay to silently ask questions about ourselves because questions help us understand what's going on within ourselves. My wish for her was that she could let go of feeling like a "bad girl" because it's not true, and I now know how harmful that belief has been.

She asked if we're happy, and I said, "Yes, we have a wonderful, meaningful, fulfilling life, and we are very lucky. Every day, we are grateful."

I explained what an essence is and that our essence is so good. She was confused by the word *essence*, but I did the best I could. I said, "We have a good heart, and we care about people a lot. We have a good nature. We know good from bad, and although we have weaknesses and downfalls like every human being, we are essentially good. We are a good girl. We are not perfect, but that's okay. Being a good girl and perfection are not synonymous. I believe there is so much perfection in being imperfect."

I told her that we grow up loving God. She knew about going to church and liked going to church, but I told her that she develops a personal relationship with God.

I felt it was important to discuss how deeply we love. Although loving intensely sometimes causes heartache, it is always worth it. In fact, it's a gift. She understood when I told her she was full of love. I told her that she sometimes would feel like she's going to burst because she has so much love inside of her.

She giggled.

I told her we had named that emotion "oodle," and, when we oodle, it means we love something so much that there is not a word to describe it. I told her that she and our children made up that version of the word.

She giggled some more.

I also explained that with our children we come up with a way to say, "I love you" or "I oodle you" without speaking, and I showed her how it's done with our eyes. She immediately understood.

She showed curiosity regarding my comments about our children. I told her we marry a wonderful man, but that idea seemed so far off to her. I told her that we have three children—and she giggled again. I told her that she grows to love riding horses with Scott, her husband, and I told her more about Scott. I told her that he is kind, hardworking, loving, and loves the mountains. I called him a cowboy.

She giggled and asked if I still like Oreos. When I replied, "Yes," we went inside our home and had Oreos dipped in milk. My visit with her felt so real that I could feel the texture of the chocolate cookies.

She showed me our bedroom; my sister's crib was still against one wall, and the bunk beds were against the other wall with their little red bedspreads. I saw my favorite pink knit skirt with matching top hanging in the closet and the black Mary Jane shoes, which my mom wanted me to keep scuff-free for special occasions, placed neatly together on the floor.

I told her that, although we are certainly capable of

dressing up, we prefer to be in jeans, and even more so in workout clothes.

We did what she called "gymnastics" together, but it was really just stretching. She giggled some more. I told her that she grows up to be athletic and always loves sports and exercise.

Then I asked if she knew the seasons, and when she nodded, I asked her if she had a favorite. "Yes, summer." When I asked her if she likes fall, she started crying, but she didn't know why.

We talked about fall and the brown grass, the colorful leaves, the football games, and the scar she gets under her chin playing football in the front yard, which causes her to miss her own birthday party. She was surprised that I knew that information.

I described autumn as beautiful, but because of what happened to us, the season makes us feel scared and unsettled. I told her that we suffer during the fall, and we don't know why until many years later.

I told her about the connection between autumn and the neighbor boy hurting us, and I told her that I knew what had happened to her many times with a stick. She listened intently as I told her that the neighbor stops hurting us when we move during kindergarten.

My four-year-old Christie thought only Carey Jones knew the secret about the neighbor boy. I told her that Carey is a friend, and I know why we created her. I also told that little girl that she would learn that she is strong enough to speak the truth and instead of hiding reality behind a make-believe person, she would learn that her voice is important. She sat quietly as I hugged her closely and protectively, which was nurturing to both the younger and older me.

Then I had to stop. She was only four years old, and my intent was to nurture this little girl. It was a powerful, rich experience. I had been successful in reaching back to my past and reprogramming certain feelings and emotions.

It was a memorable and calming self-reflection. I felt both a guttural and a calming emotion. The guttural emotion: *I ache for that little girl.* The calming emotion: *I know she's okay beyond a shadow of a doubt.*

Jerry had been right in his suggestion to me about the inner child work. Through Jerry's re-parenting exercise, I was ultimately able to reassure and reprogram my inner insecure child while impacting my adult symptoms with a deep sense of relief and calmness.

I suffered a range of symptoms from my childhood abuse because, like most children, I didn't tell anyone what was happening to me. And, like most survivors of childhood sexual abuse, I suffered from many debilitating effects of childhood sexual abuse.

When I began therapy, the thought of discussing what had happened in my early childhood had never occurred to me. I was in search of help to maintain normalcy through a tumultuous time in my household. I didn't wake up one day and decide to tell Jerry my dark secret.

However, because of my one conversation with Jerry about what happened to me when I was four and five years old, it became a subject that I could no longer ignore. Although I showed much resistance many times along the way, overcoming that resistance and the trauma released the hold that was at the root of my self-esteem.

Since that first conversation with Jerry about my early childhood sexual abuse, I have learned a great deal about the issue, how it affects survivors, and how parents and others can help prevent abuse in the first place.

We look at those subjects in parts II, III, and IV.

# Part II

*Facts about Childhood Sexual Abuse*

*Chapter 4*

# Facts and Myths about Childhood Sexual Abuse

*Not all wounds are visible.*
—Unknown

Sexual abuse is one of the most prevalent health issues for children.[9] Childhood sexual abuse can cause an array of serious mental, emotional, and physical consequences, but these effects are often buried. Like me, people often do not tell anyone about their abuse, and they don't understand the full range of the impact on their lives. Trauma-based therapeutic intervention has been shown to help people with abuse histories recover from these potential impacts, but the effects of the trauma have to be acknowledged first.[10]

Parents, teachers, neighbors, and members of all religious institutions—every adult who interacts with children professionally or as immediate or extended family members—play a role in protecting children from sexual abuse.[11]

The effects of childhood sexual abuse can be devastating,

but they do not have to be permanent.[12] There are currently more than sixty million survivors of childhood sexual abuse in our country, according to WINGS Foundation,[13] a Denver-based organization dedicated to helping adult survivors of childhood sexual abuse.

Many of these survivors continue to struggle with the untreated effects of their early abuse. Like most children, they never told anyone because of the shame they felt, because they didn't want to upset their parents, because they were afraid they wouldn't be believed, and because of other internal and external factors.

In many parts of the country, no laws protect survivors from certain types of sexual abuse, including spousal rape, sexual harassment, unwanted internet pornography, and other types of indirect and subtle forms of abuse. Statute of limitations laws may curtail or prevent survivors from getting proper justice for their abuse.

Many states are currently reevaluating their definitions and reporting standards because of the recent #MeToo and #TimesUp movements, as well as the advocacy of childhood sexual abuse survivors like Erin Merryn who is responsible for Erin's Law.

## Erin's Law

Erin's Law is named after Erin Merryn, a childhood sexual assault survivor, author, speaker, and activist. She is the founder and president of Erin's Law[14] (www.erinslaw.org)

After Erin introduced the legislation in her home state of Illinois, legislators named the bill Erin's Law, and it is now nationwide. Illinois was the first state to mandate Erin's Law.

As of July 2019, Erin's Law is legislation that is active in at least thirty-seven states, and it requires that all public schools implement a prevention-oriented child sexual abuse program teaching students in prekindergarten through twelfth grade age-appropriate techniques to recognize child sexual abuse and to tell a trusted adult. The law also requires education of school personnel about child sexual abuse and offers information to parents regarding warning signs, assistance, and support for sexually abused children and their families.[15]

Many teachers have the unique ability to be able to spot children in trouble. Parents should seriously consider any information gleaned from their children's teachers if they notice changes in behavior or acting out. There is a fine line between paranoia and alertness. We must find that fine line. We need to be vigilant because these are our children.

## Ten Myths about Childhood Sexual Abuse

There are many myths about childhood sexual abuse. One of the most effective ways parents, teachers, and other caregivers of children can prevent childhood sexual abuse is by learning the facts and the myths about childhood sexual abuse.

Myth 1: The only types of childhood sexual abuse are physical sexual acts.

False. There are many types of sexual abuse. All of them have the potential for major negative effects on children and can be detrimental to people of all ages. Acts other than physical sexual intercourse or penetration are also considered to be childhood sexual abuse. Nonphysical sexual abuse includes exhibitionism or exposing oneself to a minor; obscene phone calls, text messages, or digital interaction; and producing, owning, sharing, or showing pornographic images or movies of children. Sometimes the abuse involves only words, gestures, sexual shaming, or teasing.[16]

Myth 2: Stranger danger is the most common form of childhood sexual abuse.

False. While many children are educated from an early age to be aware of "stranger danger," the reality is that they are far more likely to be sexually abused by someone in their immediate or extended family or by someone familiar and close to the child or their family. The younger the victim, the more likely it is that the abuser is a family member. When a child under the age of six is abused, a majority of those abusers are family members.[17]

Myth 3: Perpetrators of childhood sexual abuse only target quiet, unhappy children.

False. Childhood sexual abuse incidents happen in wealthy families and poor ones, isolated families and sociable ones, two-parent households and single-parent households, and in the country and in the city. It can happen to anyone.

Myth 4: Most children who are abused have it happen the first time they are alone with the perpetrator.

False. "Engagement and grooming" is the process where the abuser gradually draws a victim into a sexual interaction and is able to maintain that contact in secrecy. Abusers often use this technique to form relationships with potential child victims and their parents prior to the abuse. In the vast majority of abuse situations, the abuser is someone within the immediate or extended family of the child or is someone they know and trust. This can result in the gradual and subtle process of grooming. However, not all incidents of childhood sexual abuse involve gradual grooming. Sometimes, an adult or older child uses violence. This is what happened to me. It was both sudden and violent.

Myth 5: Sexual abuse only occurs when victims are alone with the perpetrator.

False. Abusers can manipulate and groom both children and adults so that their actions seem ordinary or part of play. Children often feel that their parents must be okay with what is happening to them because it can happen with them present or nearby.

Myth 6: Most children blame the adult or older child who abuses them.

False. Many children are insecure or often feel like they aren't good enough. In many instances, children self-blame because they have been taught—and they believe—they are usually wrong in conflicts with adults. Abusers exploit this fact. As a result, it is not uncommon for a child to believe that she or he is somehow bad rather than the trusted person is criminally wrong. Children are often expected to defer to the wishes or demands of adults. Additionally, children are often not given the power to decide for themselves who touches them and in what manner they are touched.

When children are sexually abused, their natural sexual development is often stolen. In many cases, the child has not had a chance to sexually develop naturally, and it is not unusual for their feelings about sex to be linked to unwanted feelings like shame or disgust. As my therapist pointed out several times, since I did not associate what happened to me with sexual abuse, I did not suffer from these feelings.

Myth 7: Victims always hate their abusers.

False. Many children are abused by parents, relatives, or family friends who they love very much, which worsens the pain, shame, and long-term effects of the abuse.

Myth 8: Only adults can commit childhood sexual abuse.

False. While adults commit the vast majority of child abuse incidents involving sex, children also commit abuse against other children. In peer-to-peer childhood sexual abuse incidents, where either an older child or one or more of the victim's peers is the abuser, the incident rates are about equal for both boys and girls.[18] In many states, the age differential between the child and their peer abuser determines the legal consequences of the action.

Myth 9: Most children disclose abuse right away and tell their parents or the authorities when they are abused.

False. The vast majority of child sexual abuse incidents are never reported to authorities. A little more than one-third of all survivors ever disclose their sexual abuse, and as many as two-thirds of all survivors never tell anyone, according to researchers.[19]

In *Miss America by Day,* Marilyn Van Derbur writes, "The average child never tells … the majority fear they would be blamed or that a parent would not be able to protect them from retaliation. Many children who sought help reported that parents became hysterical or punishing or pretended that nothing had happened."[20]

Myth 10: There are obvious physical signs when a child is being abused.

False. There is no single specific sign or behavior that can be considered proof that sexual abuse has definitely occurred. It's common for the children to look and appear to be normal. Even a physical examination does not always detect signs of physical abuse.

## Conclusion

Myths about childhood sexual abuse are common among the general population, well-meaning friends, family, and educators. Dispelling the myths by learning the facts aids in prevention and/or healing from the abuse. Working with a therapist, attending support groups, talking with trusted friends, using mindfulness and other self-care techniques help in the healing process. It all boils down to awareness and being able to use the information productively.

*Chapter 5*

# How Does Childhood Sexual Abuse Happen?

> *The sad fact is that most victims maintain the secrecy around their abuse and suffer needlessly. Even sadder is when they do tell, and a parent, educator, or other adult continues the silence by not reporting the abuse.*
> —Meghan Hurley Backofen, LCSW,
> River Bridge Regional Center

There are not profiles of perpetrators of child sexual abuse. The perpetrators of childhood sexual abuse look and act just like anyone else. As we have previously noted, people who sexually abuse children can be found in families, schools, churches, recreation centers, youth sports leagues, and any other place children gather. Significantly, abusers can be—and often are—other children.[21] This was the situation in my case.

By using persuasive or manipulative methods, abusers attempt to keep the sexual abuse incidents secret. Children often feel ashamed or guilty that they could not stop the abuser or that they didn't really understand that it was wrong for the abuser to engage in the activity with them.

The pervasive secrecy around the issue is clearly one reason why many people have little or no knowledge of the frequency of sexual abuse. Often, victims of abuse, their families, and the abusers themselves are too ashamed to discuss the issue publicly. The majority of sexual abuse victims never tell because their violation was so profound that they desperately want to shield the people they are closest to from having to experience the matter as well.[22] As my therapist routinely explained to me, a child can perceive a hidden secret as a double-edged-sword. A secret can have the illusion of the promise that nothing bad will happen if that secret is not disclosed. A secret can also be the source of fear that bad things will happen if that secret is disclosed.

Speaking out about childhood sexual abuse makes it easier for many survivors to get help and feel better. Celebrities who have disclosed that they were sexually abused or molested as children include Mary Tyler Moore, Esther Williams, Oprah Winfrey, Drew Carey, Carlos Santana, Tab Hunter, Tatum O'Neal, Natalie Cole, Marie Osmond, Rosie O'Donnell, Melissa Etheridge, former Miss America Marilyn Van Derbur, Anthony Edwards, Gretchen Carlson, Sally Field, and many, many others. The publicity surrounding the disclosure of athletes like the young women on the Olympic gymnastics team also encourages other people to break the secret about their own abuse histories.

I attended a film presentation that discussed problems with young athletes, mainly women, being sufficiently protected by the US Olympic establishment. During a question and answer session afterward, one of the young women from the Olympic gymnastics team discussed her abuse and how, at least at first, she and many of the other young women who were abused did not think it was sexual abuse because it came under the guise of a medical procedure by a well-known team doctor.

## Grooming

How do perpetrators convince a child to let them be touched inappropriately? Numerous researchers have found that 80 percent of sex offenders use grooming as their primary method to facilitate the abuse.[23]

Grooming is, in essence, preparing the child for later sexual abuse. The perpetrator very slowly ingratiates a relationship with the child—and usually their parents—by developing trust and closeness.

Sexual abuse can be difficult to identify when it evolves gradually over time. Perpetrators may groom children by engaging them over a long time in activities that progress from less threatening and nonsexual to overtly sexual.[24]

Working to prevent childhood sexual abuse, Darkness to Light, in Charleston, South Carolina, lists the following red flags to be on guard for when someone is grooming your child:[25]

1. Targeting specific kids for special attention, activities, or gifts. Some offenders show a preference for a particular gender, age, or type.

2. Slowly isolating a child from family members and friends, physically and emotionally. This could include finding reasons for isolated, one-on-one interactions (sleepovers, camping trips, daily activities, etc.) or undermining relationships with parents and friends to show that "no one understands you as I do."
3. Gradually crossing physical boundaries. Full frontal hugs that last too long, making children sit in their laps, and accidental touches of private areas can all be causes for concern. In some cases, offenders have engaged in partially clothed tickle sessions, showered them with kisses, or slept in the same bed with them.
4. Encouraging a child to keep secrets from family members. The shame and fear associated with childhood sexual abuse makes it easy for offenders to enforce secrecy in this area as well, keeping abuse just between the abuser and the child.

In *Mommy, Please Read This,* Troy D. Timmons notes that abusers find common ground with the child:

> I want to find an activity or subject that is interesting to them, that allows them to relax and open up ... I can gain their trust by giving them attention. I am the person they can tell anything.[26]

This is especially appealing to children who aren't getting enough attention.

## Grooming Precedes Touch

Feather Berkower, LCSW, coauthor of *Off Limits: A Parent's Guide to Keeping Kids Safe,* encourages parents to ensure they are the ones who teach their children about sexuality instead of another child with misinformation or a potential child abuse offender. In her Parenting Safe Children workshops, Berkower notes:

> Most of the time in the US, we focus on teaching children to say no, don't touch my private parts, you're not allowed to touch me, it's my body. All of that is absolutely necessary and a child needs to know that. But how do we expect a five-year-old to look up to her uncle or coach and say "don't touch my private parts," if adults are not willing to speak up and intervene when they see concerning behavior? If adults are not modeling that type of assertive behavior because we don't want to offend or get it wrong or blame a loved one, how do we expect a child to exhibit this behavior? Parents and other adults need to know that grooming precedes touch, and it's their responsibility to stand up to misbehaving (grooming) adults on behalf of children, instead of burdening a child to be the only one to stand up to that offending adult.[27]

They work hard on getting everyone around that child to also trust them, and they most often do it right out in the open. We see behavior-pushing boundaries, like constantly tickling or touchy-feely games, and we don't say anything because it doesn't trigger us to think that it is what one normally thinks of as sexual abuse. Beware of anyone who seems inordinately physically or emotionally closer to the child than you find comfortable, including family members.

Feather Berkower, LCSW, urges parents to establish normalized conversations with their children. During her seminar, "Parenting Safe Children," she candidly asks, "Are you, as parents, willing to feel a little uncomfortable so that your children never have to?"

Many parents don't realize that having a conversation about their children's body-safety rules when hiring a babysitter, for example, is necessary and exceedingly important.

There is no single set of guidelines to teach parents how to talk to their children about sexual assault. Laura Palumbo, director of communications at the National Sexual Violence Resource Center, says that there is appropriate information to give children about sexual violence at every stage of development:[28]

> One of the biggest misconceptions is that these conversations are too advanced or harmful for children to hear about. In reality, the more information that we can give children from an early age about understanding your bodies and your boundaries and what types of touch are appropriate—not only does it give your child that information, it also lets them know that these are safe topics to talk to you about.[29]

As a parent, educator, caregiver, or any other responsible adult who is in a close relationship with a child, there are numerous ways to learn about normative sexuality development, childhood sexual abuse, minimizing potential opportunities for abusers, understanding the signs of sexual abuse, and acting responsibly. Some additional educational resources are offered in the bibliography at the end of the book.

## Risk Factors

While it is true that childhood sexual abusers look just like everyone else, and it is true that no child is immune, there are facts and situations that increase the chances that a child may be abused.

Gender is a major factor in sexual abuse. Females are five times more likely to be abused than males.[30] Boys are more often abused by someone not related by blood, and girls are more likely to be victims of incest.[31]

Age is a significant factor in sexual abuse. While there is risk for children of all ages, children are most vulnerable to abuse between the ages of seven and thirteen.[32] The median age for reported abuse is nine years old.[33] However, of the children who are sexually abused, more than 20 percent of them are sexually abused before the age of eight.[34]

Family and acquaintance child sexual abuse perpetrators work to increase a trusting relationship with children before abusing the child.[35] They choose children who they think will never tell—and even if they do tell, they think no one will believe them.

Parents can help prevent their children from being sexually abused by knowing the facts about childhood sexual abuse, teaching their children about their bodies, and explaining appropriate and inappropriate touching. The appendix by New York-based human sexuality educator Lorna Littner at the back of this book gives readers examples of normal child development by age.

Parents can also teach children about keeping secrets, the difference between a secret and a surprise, and what to do if someone is inappropriate with them.

## Signs of Childhood Sexual Abuse

There are no hard and fast rules about what constitutes normal sexual development or what behaviors might signal sexual abuse, according to the Child Welfare Information Gateway, a service of the Children's Bureau, US Department of Health and Human Services.[36] Children show a range of sexual behaviors and sexual curiosity at each developmental level, and their curiosity, interest, and experimentation may occur gradually, based on their personal development.

Children who have been sexually abused may demonstrate behaviors that are unusual, excessive, or aggressive, or the signs of the abuse may be subtle or not evident.

Child sexual abuse victims can exhibit indirect physical signs, such as anxiety, chronic stomach pain, and headaches. Emotional and behavioral signals are common among sexually abused children including "too perfect" behavior, withdrawal, fear, depression, unexplained anger, and rebellion.[37]

Medical examinations of children who have been sexually abused are almost always "normal." As noted in the previous chapter in myth 10, "It's common for the children to look and appear to be normal" when doctors examine suspected cases of abuse in children.

According to Darkness to Light, the following physical and/or emotional signs can be attributed to childhood sexual abuse and should be further investigated:

> Direct physical signs of sexual abuse are not common. However, when physical signs are present, they may include bruising, bleeding, redness and bumps, or scabs around the mouth, genitals, or anus. Urinary tract infections, sexually transmitted diseases, and abnormal vaginal or penile discharge are also warning signs (especially in younger prepubescent children). There are other indirect physical signs that include persistent or recurring pain during urination or bowel movements, wetting or soiling accidents unrelated to toilet training, sexually transmitted diseases, chronic stomach pain, or headaches.[38]

There are also many psychological and emotional symptoms that could be indicative of sexual abuse. Depression, aggression, fear of a particular person, and anxiety are just a few possible indicators. It is important to remember that any one of these behaviors or emotions does not necessarily mean that a child is being abused. However, a confluence of several of them should raise a red flag and signal the need for further investigation of their cause.

## How Often Is Childhood Sexual Abuse Reported?

Child protective service agencies investigate the majority of the child abuse incidents reported to them, and the rest are dropped for lack of adequate information or for other reasons. Of those reports investigated, only a portion meets the criteria of being "substantiated." Given the small numbers of child sexual abuse incidents that are ever reported and then substantiated, and the statistic that a child is abused in the United States every six minutes, it is no wonder that child sexual abuse is called a "silent epidemic."[39]

There are several reasons why children don't disclose the fact that they are being sexually abused. The abuse makes them feel bad about themselves or ashamed that it's happening. Many children do not want to upset their parents, and they don't tell for that reason. Other children don't tell because the abuser is someone close to the family or a family member. They could be afraid they won't be believed, they could be confused about what is happening to them, or they could have been threatened in some manner.[40] When children do disclose, delayed disclosure is common.

Marilyn Van Derbur was fifty-three years old when she disclosed information that she had been a victim of childhood sexual abuse by her father. Even then, many people didn't believe her, including her own mother. If a former Miss America is not believed, then it's easy to wonder why anyone would believe a four- or five-year-old child.

The children who do disclose that they are being abused often tell a close friend rather than an adult or someone in an authority position, but friend-to-friend disclosures do not always result in the abuse being reported. Sometimes disclosure is accidental, including when a third party observes the inappropriate behavior. In these situations, the child can feel caught and deny or minimize the extent of the abuse.

Schoolteachers and other school personnel are the main identifiers of childhood sexual abuse. They identify a majority of all identified abuse cases classified as causing harm to a child—more than any other profession or organization, including child protective services and the police.[41]

False reports of child sexual abuse made by children are rare. It is estimated that only 4 to 8 percent of child sexual abuse reports are fabricated, and when a fabricated report is made, it is most often by adults who are involved in child custody disputes.[42] According to law enforcement, children who are coached are pretty easy to spot during the investigative phase.

## Statistics

Measuring the prevalence of childhood sexual abuse can be challenging because of the different ways organizations define childhood sexual abuse. Most statistics are based on the number of "reported" incidents of childhood sexual abuse, numbers most experts believe are grossly underreported. For example, many organizations do not include peer-to-peer sexual abuse cases in their statistics or noncontact incidents of childhood sexual abuse like exhibitionism.

In 2016, the national child sexual abuse organization Darkness to Light and its authors Townsend and Rheingold concluded that a general statement about the prevalence of childhood sexual abuse is that "about one in 10 children will be sexually abused before their 18th birthday."[43] But when all forms of childhood sexual abuse are considered, the numbers grow higher. On their website, WINGS Foundation in Denver uses these figures: "1 in 4 women and 1 in 6 men, or 1 in 5 people experience some type of sexual abuse before 18 years of age."[44]

According to the sexual abuse and prevention organization Darkness to Light, at the current abuse rate, roughly four hundred thousand babies born in the United States this year will become victims of child sexual abuse before they turn eighteen—unless we do something to help stop that from happening.[45]

When children are sexually abused, they are forced to participate in and endure physical, mental, and emotional sensations and feelings that they are too young to adequately understand. Since the emotions are often too overwhelming for them, some children often repress these feelings. Over time, common emotions that result from childhood sexual abuse include numbness, shame, anger, and grief.[46]

Child sexual abuse has lasting consequences for victims. The real tragedy is that it robs children of their potential, setting into motion a chain of events and decisions that affect them throughout their lives. Substance abuse problems are a common consequence for adult survivors of child sexual abuse. Mental health problems are a common long-term consequence of child sexual abuse. Obesity and eating disorders are more common in women who have a history of child sexual abuse.[47]

Mental health coordinator Meghan Hurley Backofen,

LCSW, who works with River Bridge Regional Center in Glenwood Springs, Colorado, states:

> Many people live with untreated posttraumatic stress, which can include pervasive thoughts about the abuse, avoidance of abuse reminders, anger, shame, guilt, and a decreased sense of self-worth. Many childhood traumas (exposure to natural disasters, accidents, and injuries) are resolved naturally through talking about the event and getting support. The sad fact is that most victims maintain the secrecy around their abuse and suffer needlessly. Even sadder is when they do tell, and a parent, educator, or other adult continues the silence by not reporting the abuse. This prevents the child from getting mental health treatment and communicates to the child that the offender didn't do something wrong enough to be in trouble. Reporting the abuse, and breaking the silence in which sexual abuse thrives, greatly helps a child move out of being a victim of posttraumatic stress to becoming a survivor.

The degree of trauma a child may experience can also be affected by the support of other family members after disclosure, the closeness of the relationship between the child and their abuser, whether threats or violence were part of the incident and grooming process, and if the child purposely disclosed and the abuse stopped as a result. Many children are confused by what is happening or don't have the words to be able to describe concretely what is happening.

# Part III

*For Survivors*

## Chapter 6

# Adult Survivors of Childhood Sexual Abuse

*Loving ourselves through the process of owning our story is the bravest thing we'll ever do.*
—Brené Brown

As we have noted before, childhood sexual abuse can cause a range of emotional, psychological, and physical effects and behaviors. Unfortunately, many survivors share similar consequences as a result of their childhood traumas. But each survivor's experience and their story are different, as is mine.

Childhood abuse encompasses far more than bruises and broken bones. Physical child abuse can include serious physical problems and long-lasting scars, but the emotional effects of child abuse are far more serious.[48]

Every type of childhood abuse and neglect leaves lasting scars upon a child. Children who undergo proper therapy and treatment for child abuse are able to work through some of their lasting emotional problems.

Effects of childhood abuse may include:

- lack of trust
- impaired brain development
- inability to engage in fulfilling relationships
- poor physical health
- poor emotional and mental health
- cognitive difficulties
- social differences
- juvenile delinquency and adult criminality
- abusive behaviors
- feeling "too damaged to love"
- low self-worth
- feelings of worthlessness
- difficulties with emotional regulation
- depression
- anxiety
- anger
- alcoholism
- drug addiction
- suicidal thoughts and behaviors[49]

## Common Survivor Emotions

Survivors of childhood sexual abuse may feel some of the following emotions:

### Shame

Most survivors feel ashamed and guilty about the abuse they suffered as children, which was certainly true for me.

Survivors feel they should have stopped the abuse—even though the abuser is physically much more powerful than the child and may resort to violence or threaten violence to get what they want.[50]

Throughout my childhood, the truth behind my desire to be a "good girl" stemmed from feeling dirty, ashamed, and bad. I was unable to articulate these feelings, and I also was not even consciously aware of them, so I felt personal disgust and self-loathing for years until those feelings were uncovered during therapy.

In, *Unspoken Legacy,* Claudia Black, PhD, states:

> One of the hallmarks of shame is this ongoing self-deprecating inner dialogue, which rarely gets outwardly expressed. Some clinicians and researchers describe shame as a feeling, but my experience as a therapist has taught me that shame causes people to actually disconnect from their feelings and become numb to them. Shame is not so much an emotion as it is an emotional block. The greater someone's shame, the more numb he or she tends to become.
>
> When someone begins the all-important work of healing his or her trauma, inherent in the process will be the healing of shame.[51]

## Fear

Childhood sexual abuse is frightening and causes stress long after the experience or experiences have ceased. Anxiety, tension, panic attacks, and phobias are common effects of childhood sexual abuse.[52]

Fear, anxiety, and always being on guard are normal responses to trauma and childhood sexual abuse.[53]

When I was four and five years old and was repeatedly sexually assaulted by the neighborhood boy, I began to fear going outside to play. I also began to avoid playing outdoors. Instead, I created tea parties, which became a favorite activity of mine. If possible, I would stay in my room and be comforted by my imaginary friend, Carey Jones.

Learning to recognize and work with fear is an important part of our recovery.[54] Recovery involves being able to recognize fear while not becoming immobilized by it.

## Anger

Physical, emotional, or sexual abuse in childhood can interrupt the normal development of skills needed for healthy emotional management and relationship building. Children exposed to such behavior learn that anger and aggression can be used in relationships to communicate, establish dominance, exert control, solve problems, and resolve conflict.[55]

For some survivors, it is easier to feel angry than to feel the more vulnerable emotions of sadness or hurt. When anger masks our true feelings and emotions, the repercussions to our health and lifestyle are often devastating. Anger, unlike other emotions, inherently feels powerful. Therefore, it's easy to be swept up in anger when you begin to feel vulnerable.[56]

Sometimes, anger is directed inward because many survivors believe they could have done or said something to stop the abuse from happening. These reactions are normal and understandable responses to trauma and surviving childhood sexual abuse. It is important for survivors to be gentle with themselves. They are not at fault. They are not bad.[57]

As a child, I remember having what I now know was misdirected anger with a sometimes-quick temper. Occasionally, when I became angry, I didn't know why, which is a horrible feeling.

Inevitably, I turned anger into self-disgust, probably because I was set on being a good girl. Sometimes, the confusion turned to self-sabotage in the form of emotional and unconscious eating. I learned that awareness and acknowledgment were paramount before I could successfully conquer self-sabotage.

As I grew older, I repressed anger. In fact, many who know me claim to have never seen that trait in me. Although there are effective methods to direct and calm one's anger, denying the emotion completely is not one of them.

It wasn't until I was in therapy as an adult that some previous emotions made sense. At some point in therapy, I remember an uncomfortable discussion with Jerry when he asked me to try to gather and succinctly write my candid thoughts toward my perpetrator. Reluctantly, I agreed. Reluctantly, because I knew I would have to authentically get in touch with painful feelings that had built up for more than forty years, and I dreaded that idea.

I found that giving myself permission to be angry was difficult, which was a valuable insight. But, as I let the memories flow and allowed myself to feel uncensored anger, shame, and grief, the assignment developed into a scathing letter, and I expressed my long overdue anger for what my perpetrator had done to me as a child. It was, perhaps, when

I began to stop minimizing my personal childhood sexual abuse.

## Grief/Loss

Many adult survivors of childhood sexual abuse have lost some part of their childhood to that earlier abuse. Many children are forced to grow up too soon as they deal with emotions and experiences they aren't ready for. They are forced to turn off a sense of curiosity, playfulness, and spontaneity in order to manage the impact of the trauma they experienced. When we grieve these losses, it is important to frame the losses in terms of appropriate responsibility instead of self-blame.[58]

As a direct result of my self-blame, I became an emotional eater, and no matter how much food I put inside my tummy, there was still an insatiable void.

## Depression

Depression is a mood disorder that negatively affects how someone feels, thinks, and acts. Emotional and mental health problems are often the first consequence of depression and can be a sign of childhood sexual abuse. Children who are sexually abused are at significantly greater risk for later post-traumatic stress, anxiety, and depression.[59] These psychological problems can lead to significant disruptions in normal development and often have a lasting impact, leading to dysfunction and distress well into adulthood.

According to WINGS Foundation:

Depression is familiar to many survivors. It's a low-energy state that leaves people feeling emotionally flat, socially disconnected, and mentally disengaged. Depression can also be a high-energy state, as it takes a lot of energy to maintain depression.[60]

Depression often shows up in a survivor's life when there is a need to express other emotions like anger, sadness, grief, outrage, or disappointment, but they are unable to do so. The unconscious mind often resorts to depression as a way to push down or suppress these painful and uncomfortable feelings of hopelessness, pessimism, guilt, worthlessness, or helplessness. Depression can create a vicious cycle because it isolates us from friends and relationships, which leads to more separation from the world, which makes us feel worse and ultimately more depressed.[61]

One of the most powerful tools for working with depression is to separate it from who we are as people. When we feel disconnected, unmotivated, or helpless from depression, it is important that we not mistake it for who we really are. Depression does not define us. If depression persists or continues to return, a therapist or mental health professional can assist in dealing with this issue.

My personal therapy proved to be instrumental in discovering the link between autumn and my childhood sexual abuse. Throughout years of enduring the psychological pain that autumn brought, I learned that it was important to have a cognitive understanding of the difference between the reality of the fall malaise and the fear that I might suffer from the fall malaise.

Before understanding the relationship between fall and my childhood sexual abuse, I just knew fall was a lonely, sad time for me. I needed to distinguish between the old memories, which occurred in autumn, and the present-day reality. Anticipatory fears can trigger emotions that are essentially identical to the subject being feared. I learned that it's necessary to understand the difference between anticipatory fear and real trauma. Realizing it was the subconscious memories and emotions that affected me—and not the characteristics of fall—was a golden nugget of knowledge.

At one point, when I was struggling with the onset of autumn, Jerry suggested that it might be time to make an appointment to start antidepressant medication to combat the feelings, which I had done for many previous autumns.

However, that year, I wanted to make a change. I announced that I didn't want to be on an antidepressant. I wanted to experience and feel everything. With Jerry's help, I was determined to figure out the missing pieces and unsettling emotions about fall.

Jerry compassionately agreed to help me with one caveat. With my best interest in mind, he asked me to be open-minded if he deemed that I would benefit from an antidepressant during the autumn season. I accepted with complete trust. We worked hard, and I got through that fall season without antidepressants.

However, we also made a major breakthrough that fall: we discovered that my sexual abuse occurred during the autumn months. It was as if my body had been remembering and re-remembering the abuse each year. The intellectual insight was profound, but I also learned over time that emotional insight would take much longer to comprehend.

I am frequently reminded by thoughts and behaviors that doing "the work" isn't like putting a check mark in the box, and poof, it's gone, forever. The work requires one day at a time of reaching a positive level of removing any debilitating thoughts that affect behaviors and mental state.

Survivors often feel they must have been at fault, and it's hard for them to understand that someone they know, trust, or even love hurt them. For survivors, letting go of shame and guilt and placing it on the person responsible for the abuse is a step forward in the healing process.

In *Surviving Childhood Sexual Abuse,* Carolyn Ainscough and Kay Toon describe how abusers get children to do what they want:

> Abusers rarely need to use physical force to coerce children into sexual relationships; they exert power in other ways ... Adults and older children are also able to manipulate the child's feelings. They can use threats and promises to gain access to the child's body and keep the child quiet.[62]

As we noted, the long-term effects of child abuse impact a child's psychological, behavioral, social, and developmental potential. The earlier the abuse is stopped and treatment begun, the more resiliency the child learns and the better the outcome.[63]

Recognizing negative emotions in our lives—shame, anger, grief, fear, depression, and anxiety—is painful, but it moves us forward in the healing process. If we stuff emotions inside of us and don't let them come out, they don't go away. In fact, it only makes them harder to deal with when we decide to eventually work on these feelings willingly; otherwise, circumstances eventually force the subject to the surface.[64]

*Chapter 7*

# Ego Defenses, Coping Strategies, and Muting the Pain

*Vulnerability sounds like truth and feels like courage. Truth and courage aren't always comfortable, but they're never weakness.*
—Brené Brown

## Ego Defenses and Coping Strategies

Through therapy, I have learned the important roles ego defenses and coping behaviors play in our lives. All human beings regularly utilize some form of ego defense to escape uncomfortable situations when in psychological pain, and survivors of childhood sexual abuse use a variety of coping behaviors to manage or tolerate the abuse when it is happening. Both ego defense mechanisms and coping strategies reduce the arousal of negative emotions, and both processes are attempts to adapt to psychological and physical stress and trauma. Defense mechanisms are unconscious processes, and coping behaviors are conscious processes.

## Ego Defenses

Ego defenses are usually benign, temporary, and not problematic. However, when they interfere significantly with functioning, having a clear awareness of them is critical. Knowing why we use them—and how they distort reality—can provide powerful healing insights. Psychotherapy and personal mindfulness aim to decode and understand ego defense mechanisms and motivations.

We all use dozens of these defense mechanisms throughout our lives, but we are mostly unaware of them. According to my therapist, some commonly used ego defenses are:

- Repression: Removing threatening thoughts from our conscious awareness. For example, not admitting to ourselves that we are pleased when a rival suffers a misfortune.
- Projection: Attributing negative thoughts or impulses to others rather than oneself. For example, believing another wants to hurt us rather than facing the fact that we would like to hurt them.
- Displacement: Expressing negative thoughts or acts, whereby others become safe targets. For example, yelling at the dog rather than yelling at your boss.
- Regression: Reverting to earlier, primitive expressions of frustration. For example, pounding on the wall like a child rather than appropriately verbalizing the frustration.
- Sublimation: Expressing a socially inappropriate impulse via a socially acceptable one. For example,

someone with an excessive need for control becomes a successful administrator.
- Denial: Refusal to face uncomfortable thoughts. For example, a person with terminal cancer might deny that they are going to die.
- Compensation: Counterbalancing perceived weaknesses through emphasis in other areas. For example, emphasizing athletic skills as a balance for academic weakness.
- Dissociation: A lack of connection in a person's thoughts, memory, and sense of identity. For example, getting lost in fantasy rather than dealing with a current uncomfortable situation.

## Using Defense Mechanisms

Using defense mechanisms as a child might be a positive asset because it allowed you to get through severe trauma, but as an adult, you can choose to learn new behaviors and new defense mechanisms that might be even more beneficial in your life.

> *I'm still coping with my trauma, but coping by trying to find different ways to heal it rather than hide it.*
> —Clemantine Wamariya

## Types of Coping Mechanisms

Coping skills effectively change thoughts, feelings, and actions so that we can manage stressful situations, specific external demands, and/or internal demands.

Among the more commonly used adaptive coping mechanisms are:

- Support: Talking about a stressful event with a supportive person can be an effective way of managing stress. Seeking external support instead of self-isolating and internalizing the effects of stress can greatly reduce the negative effects of a difficult situation.
- Relaxation: Any number of relaxing activities can help people cope with stress. Relaxing activities may include practicing meditation, progressive muscle relaxation or other calming techniques, sitting in nature, or listening to soft music.
- Problem-solving: This coping mechanism involves identifying a problem that is causing stress and then developing and putting into action some potential solutions for effectively managing it.
- Humor: Making light of a stressful situation may help people maintain perspective and prevent the situation from becoming overwhelming.
- Physical activity: Exercise can serve as a natural and healthy form of stress relief. Running, yoga, swimming, walking, dance, team sports, and many other types of physical activities can help people cope with stress and the aftereffects of traumatic events.

All of these coping mechanisms can be viewed as strengths because they allow a survivor to not be overwhelmed by the abusive experience.[65]

A short list of common maladaptive coping mechanisms includes:

- Escape: To cope with anxiety or stress, some people withdraw from friends and become socially isolated. They may absorb themselves in solitary activities such as watching television, reading, or spending time online.
- Unhealthy self-soothing: Some self-soothing behaviors are healthy in moderation but may turn into unhealthy addictions if they become habits to self-soothe. Some examples of unhealthy self-soothing are overeating, binge drinking, and excessive use of the internet or video games.
- Numbing: Some self-soothing behaviors may become numbing behaviors. When a person engages in numbing behavior, they are often aware of what they are doing and seek out an activity that will help them drown out or override their distress. People may seek to numb their stress with junk food, excessive alcohol use, or drugs.
- Compulsions and risk-taking: Stress can cause some people to seek an adrenaline rush through compulsive or risk-taking behaviors such as gambling, unsafe sex, experimenting with drugs, theft, or reckless driving.
- Self-harm: People may engage in self-harming behaviors to cope with extreme stress or trauma.

Everyone copes with painful, stressful, or uncontrollable situations differently. Some children deal with childhood sexual abuse with few psychological difficulties as children, and they go on to live lives with little or no psychological effects as adults.[66]

The nature and severity of the abuse, the types of acts committed, the use of physical force, the relationship of the abuser to the abused, and the support provided to the child by family members and others are all factors in survivors' long-term functioning.[67]

Survivors of childhood sexual abuse have complex and sometimes very creative ways of coping. Some of these methods are productive and positive, and some are less positive or even destructive. As survivors, it's important to discover the coping skills used as a child during childhood sexual abuse and the skills that continue to be used as an adult. If we keep the positive behaviors and replace the self-destructive negative behaviors with healthier ones, we continue the healing process.[68]

Developing and maintaining healthy coping skills is important for living a fulfilling life. Unfortunately, when we were surviving the abuse as children, we may have developed skills that were not helpful to us in the long run. They may be skills that we unconsciously created—or they were the best we could think of at the time—but in the long term, they did not positively affect our lives.

Using effective coping skills in our lives decreases the drama because we are thinking about our choices with adult minds rather than reacting to the trauma of the hurt inner child's mind and thinking automatically.[69]

## Carey Jones as a Defense Mechanism

As a young child, the primary defense mechanism I used to comfort myself was to invent a wondrous imaginary friend.

I now know that as a result of repeated sexual abuse, I fashioned my very first ego defense mechanism in Carey Jones. Although this ego defense mechanism was immature and primitive in nature, Carey was created when I was four to deal with the fact that I hadn't told anybody what was happening to me. I desperately needed someone to know what was going on—someone who would not consider me dirty, shameful, or bad.

I was just a young child, but I knew that Carey Jones served a monumental purpose for me. Even though I didn't know anything about sexuality then, I knew what was happening to me was wrong, and I was frightened. I somehow believed that if my family determined that Carey wasn't real, they would also discover my horrific secret of what was happening to me.

I have titled the book after Carey Jones because she played such a significant role in helping me through my times of sexual abuse. However, the truth is that while Carey served a wonderful, therapeutic purpose for me at the time, she was also a problematic defense mechanism.

Creating Carey prevented me from having to further develop other relationships that I could look to for compassion, assistance, or protection, such as my parents. Instead, I created a fantasy in Carey Jones, and she, alone, provided me with comfort about my childhood sexual abuse. Although I remain grateful for Carey Jones, her existence ultimately proved a barrier for me seeking help from my family. She also contributed to my broader isolation, adding to the entangled web of secrecy and shame I felt inside.

I still feel much affection for Carey. After a lifetime of only feeling her supportive aspects, I grew and learned something about myself when I explored how her existence limited my ability to heal.

I do wonder how my life would have changed if I had not created her. As Freud noted, a major goal of therapy is to make the unconscious conscious. When one is aware of the reasons behind behaviors, it is easier to make healthier choices. Learning about the various positive and negative aspects of Carey Jones remains a reminder for me that many of the defenses erected by the survivors of childhood sexual abuse can be double-edged swords, and that understanding those defenses can be critical to recovery. The same defenses, such as unconscious eating, that allow us to survive the abuse as children can be crippling when we still use them as adults.

## Being a Good Girl

A second defense mechanism I created in my childhood was my obsession with being considered a good girl by others. That defense mechanism never worked, and no matter how many times I extracted the "Christie is a good girl" comment from my parents and others, I believed the opposite.

Eventually, soliciting reaffirmation that I was a good little girl morphed into a personality characteristic of needing to please. I tried to not offend or challenge anyone, and I was compelled to follow others' ideas of how I should act. It doesn't take much imagination to understand how this abject fear of being thought of badly colored my existence.

Like many survivors of childhood sexual abuse, I used a variety of defensive mechanisms to deal with unwanted thoughts and feelings. Through therapy, I eventually began to understand the defense mechanisms I used to escape my abuse. I learned I no longer needed these defense mechanisms to cover shame for what someone else did to me.

## Dissociation

Dissociation is when people mentally or emotionally disconnect from a difficult, usually traumatic, situation.

The most common use of dissociation involves mentally absenting yourself from what is presently happening. For example, during a rape, the victim may experience just blanking out or feeling as if the act is being viewed from some distant place.

Dissociation ranges from simply not hearing what is being said in conversation to forgetting or repressing a difficult or traumatic event.[70]

Dissociation is a formal psychiatric diagnosis. However, in common parlance, it simply refers to zoning out or doing things without realizing you are doing them. Dissociation ranges from mild and not problematic—getting lost in a book or movie or daydreaming while driving—to serious mental disorders. These identity disorders, such as dissociative identity disorder, refer to a condition when you completely suppress a whole personality to become another personality, or multiple, extremely different personalities, with all of them residing in the same body at the same time.

In abusive situations, because they cannot escape, children will leave their bodies as much as they can.[71] They ignore, repress, and pay absolutely no attention to what is happening to their bodies, focus on some other thought, or simply blank out.

When I first described the instances of my sexual assaults in therapy, I described myself as a third party looking on, like I was floating above the scene and watching it happen to me to avoid feeling, to avoid being there, and to avoid ever being aware of what was happening to me. In therapy, when I described what happened to me, it was as if I was being re-traumatized:

> It was as if the neighbor boy caught me all over again. That's when everything during my therapy appointment often changed ... I could visualize how he would hold my arm behind my back so I was immobile, and I could visualize a pink outfit. I could picture pretty much everything about the surroundings, but it was as if I was looking on to the scene, not a part of it. I just turned off, so I wouldn't feel anything, just like I had done during the abuse.

This has been a long process, and I have worked to not dissociate during uncomfortable situations, specifically during therapy. I know that the neighbor boy cannot hurt me, and I consciously know that I cannot fill a void by emotional eating. But many times during therapy, I mentally left (not physically). I don't know where I went, but I went blank and mute, and I was incapable of communication. It is painful to think about now, but it was part of my process.

Dissociation is an unconscious defense mechanism that served me as an abused child to avoid the pain of the anal rapes. However, as an adult, it can prevent me from facing reality by blocking out painful situations—literally not remembering them. Now, with awareness, I know dissociation no longer serves me. Instead, it is an unhealthy avoidance mechanism for me.

As a child, it may have been a useful mechanism during a traumatic time, but as my therapist counseled, as an adult, it may be more useful for us to stay in the conversation or action that is happening since it leads us to deal with difficult events in more positive and more effective ways.

During the process of therapy, the times when I gained much insight were mixed with times filled with frustration. Sometimes, I experienced post-session confusion, unhappiness, and dissatisfaction, which usually resulted from dealing with heavy issues yet to be understood and resolved. For me, freezing (one form of dissociation) happened when resistance to an issue was higher.

My personal experience includes my periodic use of many forms of dissociation. I would be in a session and suddenly realize I had not heard, or couldn't remember, what had been said, or even what topic was being discussed. Sometimes, I would just curl into a ball and disappear. Other times, I could not stop babbling about random unrelated topics. Many times, I could simply not talk at all, or I felt lost in confusion—both of which often produced tears.

Dissociation happened frequently enough that Jerry and I decided that I should begin taping my therapy sessions. Then, I would listen to the tapes away from therapy, usually multiple times. I found myself amazed by how I acted during the sessions and how much I had completely missed in some sessions.

Taping the sessions proved to be extremely valuable for my healing. I have retained the recordings and still periodically listen to them, and I continue to learn from them.

## Muting the Pain

Adult survivors of abuse often try to self-medicate with drugs or alcohol to dull the painful memories. Helping individuals recover from addiction often means dealing with the underlying childhood trauma.[72]

Many childhood sexual abuse survivors struggle with addictive and compulsive behaviors. Addictive behaviors are actions people engage in as the result of physical or psychological dependence, and compulsive behaviors are actions people do in order to lessen anxiousness. In both cases, these behaviors serve to distract us from our feelings and may be ways of externally medicating or lessening our pain instead of dealing with it directly.[73]

Changing or eliminating destructive behaviors can be a difficult process because we often have two very strong contradictory feelings inside our heads about our addictions and compulsions. It's common for survivors to feel embarrassed or ashamed of the addiction or compulsion because it makes us feel bad about ourselves, which is sometimes known as *toxic shame.* The second feeling comes (often at the same time) because the addiction or compulsion makes us feel good and helps us temporarily forget about the pain of our trauma. The addiction or compulsion feels like a friend who is always available to us.[74]

Our addictions and compulsions are elaborate defense mechanisms that helped and protected us from painful circumstances, but we no longer need them in recovery.[75]

To recover from the effects of childhood sexual abuse, survivors must learn how to feel again. To help survivors with addictive or compulsive drinking and using drugs, many work with Alcoholics Anonymous (AA) and Narcotics Anonymous (NA). Both organizations have hotlines in cities and towns across the country, and they have meetings hosted by recovering addicts and alcoholics who will assist in your efforts to become clean and sober.

## Eating Disorders

Eating disorders describe illnesses that are characterized by irregular eating habits and severe distress or concern about body weight or shape.

Eating disorders can develop during any stage in life, but they typically appear during the teen years or young adulthood. Eating disturbances include both inadequate or excessive food intake that can ultimately damage an individual's well-being. The most common forms of eating disorders include anorexia nervosa, bulimia nervosa, and binge eating disorder and affect both females and males.[76]

Eating disorders commonly coexist with other conditions, such as anxiety disorders, substance abuse, or depression.[77]

Obesity and eating disorders are more common in women who have a history of child sexual abuse. Some women who have suffered from childhood sexual abuse may consciously or subconsciously decide that they will gain pounds as a defense mechanism to ward off any future males' sexualized attention toward them.[78]

For many people, compulsive eating is a way to suppress emotions and avoid feeling pain.[79]

That certainly was the case for me—even though I did not know that as a four-year-old who suffered from repeated incidents of trauma. After I cleaned myself up from the sexual assaults, I would always go to the kitchen. In my pain, I would attempt to comfort myself—or nurture myself—to fill a void by eating whatever was around until there was no more room in my tummy.

In *Surviving Childhood Sexual Abuse*, Carolyn Ainscough and Kay Toon state that at least half the women who have eating disorders suffered from incidents of childhood sexual abuse:

> Sexual abuse is forced on children by the power and authority an adult or older child has over them. Children may also feel powerless to resist because of threats or actual physical violence from the abuser or because they feel very confused about what is happening to them. When people feel powerless and out of control, a thing they can control is their own body. Small children who are being abused often overeat, refuse

to eat or wet or soil themselves. These are body functions they alone can control, and which adults cannot take control. If feelings of powerlessness and loss of control develop as the child grows up, the body may again become a means of regaining some control.[80]

One of the ways to address eating problems is to make the distinction between psychological appetite and physical hunger. Physical hunger occurs when our bodies need food for energy to get us through the day. Without food, our bodies do not have the energy they need to survive; in particular, our brains don't have the blood sugar they need to make good decisions. Psychological appetite has to do with our emotional relationship with food. Our culture, our families, and our own personal histories influence it, and it is quite different from physical hunger.[81]

As we recover, we want to find ways of gaining mastery over our feelings that do not hurt our bodies. We want to use food properly, function the best, and have the resources and energy to more skillfully focus our attention on taking care of ourselves in other ways.[82]

## Self-Harm

Self-harm or self-injury can be one of the ways we work to separate or distance ourselves from traumatic memories. Self-harm can manifest in different ways like cutting or burning ourselves, pulling out hair, or even ingesting toxic materials. People who purposely injure themselves are typically looking for relief from extremely intense emotions. Survivors can be looking to relieve different symptoms by self-harming.[83]

Survivors often feel like they have no control. The belief that one lacks control over what happens to them—and that they are powerless—invokes fear. At the time of the abuse experienced in childhood, there was no control. During periods of self-harm, survivors are able to influence the type of pain and how much pain they experience. It is extremely important to many survivors that they gain a sense of control over their lives. When they self-harm, there is evidence of that control.[84]

There are physical and emotional connections between self-harm and childhood sexual abuse. There is often an absence of pain during the act of self-injury, which is like the absence of sensation that often occurs during the abuse. Within the body's own defense system, natural opiates numb the trauma and have the effect of numbing the emotions, so that little may be felt and realized consciously.[85]

## Conclusion

My defense mechanisms and coping behaviors are common among those who have suffered childhood sexual abuse. Hopefully my story will provide others with motivation to examine their own defense mechanisms and coping behaviors, gain control over them, and foster long-term healing.

For multiple kinds of trauma, a goal for healing is to recognize and replace self-destructive behaviors with productive ones. Through therapy, I learned that I was unconsciously using the defense mechanisms of creating Carey

Jones and always needing to be thought of as a good girl to manage my childhood trauma. I consciously coped with my earlier childhood sexual abuse by eating emotionally and escaping from the reality of every fall season.

In therapy, I was able to learn how my defense mechanisms and coping behaviors served a purpose when I was being sexually abused as a child. I was also able to learn that, as an adult, these mechanisms and behaviors no longer served a useful purpose in my life. Although painful memories, symptoms, and damaging defenses may remain, personal growth and recovery can also happen with the very first step of awareness.

## Chapter 8

# Trauma and Posttraumatic Stress

*All emotions, even those that are suppressed and unexpressed, have physical effects. Unexpressed emotions tend to stay in the body like small ticking time bombs—they are illnesses in incubation.*
—Marilyn Van Derbur, former Miss America and incest survivor

When people experience severe psychological distress following any terrible or life-threatening event, they may suffer from trauma. Sufferers may develop emotional disturbances such as extreme anxiety, anger, sadness, survivor's guilt, acute stress disorder, or posttraumatic stress.[86]

It is common for people who have been through a traumatic experience to have ongoing problems with sleep or physical pain, encounter turbulence in their personal and professional relationships, or feel a sense of diminished self-worth due to the overwhelming amount of stress they are feeling.[87]

Although the instigating event of the trauma may overpower your coping resources available at the time, it is nevertheless possible to develop healthy ways of coping with trauma and diminishing its effects.[88]

According to the American Psychological Association:

> Trauma is an emotional response to a terrible event like an accident, rape, or natural disaster. Immediately after the event, shock and denial are typical. Longer-term reactions include unpredictable emotions, flashbacks, reactions to triggers, avoidance of situations that remind one of the events (for example, not going into a room where the abuse occurred), negative changes in beliefs and feelings, and strained relationships. While these feelings are normal, some people have difficulty moving on with their lives.[89]

Traumatic events of any type greatly affect a child, and it is especially common for a child who has suffered from childhood sexual abuse to partially or completely forget about what happened to them. Our brains process memories in ways to protect us. If we cannot remember the trauma, we can at some level live as if it didn't happen. About half of all survivors experience some memory difficulty. Survivors may have absolutely no memories of sexual abuse or only incomplete memories.[90]

According to Judith Herman's groundbreaking work, *Trauma and Recovery*, repeated trauma in adult life erodes the structure of the personality already formed, but repeated trauma in childhood forms and deforms the personality.[91]

## Effects of Trauma

How individuals react to trauma has been an important field of study since at least World War I when combat veterans were analyzed for the effects of the trauma they suffered during combat, and new treatments were developed to treat them. Similarly, the trauma caused by natural disasters around the world, and its effect on the humans suffering through these events, has also been well documented. However, it wasn't until the emergence of the women's movement in the early 1970s that sexual trauma—caused by rape or sexual abuse—began to be taken more seriously. Not until the women's liberation movement of the 1970s was it recognized that the most common posttraumatic disorders are those not of men in war but of women in civilian life.[92]

It was the study of men in combat that led to the concept of posttraumatic stress disorder (PTSD), and mental health professionals eventually recognized similar PTSD syndromes in survivors of rape, domestic battery, and incest.[93]

According to the Mayo Clinic, the effects of trauma can create the symptoms of posttraumatic stress disorder. Symptoms can vary over time or vary from person to person.

Posttraumatic stress disorder (PTSD) symptoms are generally grouped into four types:

- Intrusive memories are recurrent, unwanted distressing memories of the traumatic event.
- Avoidance is trying to avoid thinking or talking about a traumatic event.

- Negative changes in thinking and mood include negative thoughts about you, other people, or the world.
- Changes in physical and emotional reactions include being easily startled or having trouble concentrating.[94]

PTSD is a normal reaction to being exposed to very abnormal or traumatic experiences that in some way threaten our lives. Studies have revealed that childhood sexual abuse is traumatizing and can result in symptoms comparable to symptoms of war-related trauma.[95]

On numerous occasions throughout my course of therapy, my therapist spoke of posttraumatic stress in reference to my ongoing symptoms and resulting self-beliefs. Repeatedly, I stated that I didn't "deserve" to use the term PTS. I did not believe that my history was worthy of the association with PTS. I was wrong.

Acute stress disorder (ASD) is a mental disorder that can occur in the first month following a trauma. The symptoms that define ASD overlap with those of posttraumatic stress. One difference is that a PTSD diagnosis cannot be given until the stress symptoms have lasted for at least one month.

PTSD symptoms can vary in intensity over time. There may be more PTSD symptoms when stressed in general or when reminders of your abuse occur. A car backfiring might cause someone to relive a combat experience—or a report on the news about a sexual assault might remind someone of their own assault.

## Long-Term Effects

Dr. David Finkelhor, a notable and often-quoted expert, has researched and reported on the long-term effects of childhood sexual abuse with his partner, Dr. Angela Browne. In their extensive research, Finkelhor and Browne found that childhood sexual abuse incidents create trauma in children, and the long-term effects of that abuse are categorized in four trauma dynamics: traumatic sexualization, betrayal, stigmatization, and powerlessness.[96]

These dynamics alter children's cognitive and emotional orientation to the world and create trauma by distorting a children's self-concept, worldview, and affective capacities.[97]

According to Finkelhor and Browne:

> Traumatic sexualization refers to a process in which a child's sexuality (including both sexual feelings and sexual attitudes) is shaped in a developmentally inappropriate and interpersonally dysfunctional fashion as a result of sexual abuse.[98]

Many survivors struggle with sexual issues as adults because of their earlier childhood sexual abuse. My therapist explained that early sexualization or sexual trauma could negatively rewire a child's brain, resulting in a multitude of results for survivors. I thought what happened to me was horrible, but I didn't connect it with sex or sexual assault until years later in therapy. Not connecting the anal rape to something sexual probably served me since it did not compromise my adult sexuality.

For many survivors, it's common to feel shame or guilt because their bodies reacted normally when they were touched in a sexual way, and they may have felt feelings of enjoyment. These feelings are normal reactions to the abnormal situation of being sexually abused.[99] They do not equate with "consent" or "wanting it."

Betrayal refers to the dynamic by which children discover that someone on whom they were vitally dependent has caused them harm. This may occur in a variety of ways in a molestation experience. For example, in the course of abuse or its aftermath, children may come to the realization that a trusted person has manipulated them through lies or misrepresentations about moral standards.[100]

The dynamic of powerlessness distorts children's sense of their ability to control their lives. Children's attempts to cope with the world through these distortions may result in some of the behavioral problems that are commonly noted in victims of child sexual abuse.[101] The trauma in this dynamic may be increased if the child has tried to tell someone but was not supported or understood.

The support of a non-offending parent needs to be in place in order for a child to heal from trauma in a timely fashion. Former Miss America Marilyn Van Derbur has described her emotions of feeling more anger toward her mother than her father. Although her father committed the immense betrayal by sexually abusing Marilyn for thirteen years, she felt even more betrayal from her mother, who chose not to believe her when she did disclose she had been a longtime victim of incest.

Personally, I can relate to the feelings of betrayal and

powerlessness that were caused by my childhood sexual abuse. I felt betrayed by my predator. He was a neighborhood boy who had never given any reason to think he would harm someone. The fear he instilled in me was paralyzing, and I felt powerless to do anything about it.

Stigmatization refers to the negative connotations (badness, shame, and guilt) that are communicated to the child around the experiences and then become incorporated into the child's self-image. The dynamic of stigmatization distorts a child's sense of their own value and worth.[102]

These negative meanings are communicated in many ways. They can come directly from the abuser, who may blame the victim for the activity, demean the victim, or furtively convey a sense of shame about the behavior. Pressure for secrecy from the offender can also convey powerful messages of shame and guilt. Stigmatization is also reinforced by attitudes that the victim infers or hears from other persons in the family or community. Stigmatization may grow out of the child's prior knowledge or sense that the activity is considered deviant and taboo, and it is certainly reinforced if, after disclosure, people react with shock or hysteria or blame the child for what has transpired.[103]

Even though I was only four and five years old at the time, I knew what the neighbor boy was doing to me was bad, and I felt a sense of shame and guilt because of that.

## Healing Trauma

People cannot heal until they acknowledge what has happened to them and feel safe to tell their story.

But healing doesn't mean that the survivor is completely over the symptoms of the trauma or the symptoms of posttraumatic stress. Many of the symptoms may reoccur during times of stress or instances where a sound, smell, or anniversary date reminds the survivor of the earlier abuse. Healing is a process, and the healing comes when symptoms occur and the survivor is able to mitigate or work around the symptoms.[104]

In *The Body Keeps the Score*, Dr. Bessel Van Der Kolk explains how research and imaging tools help us:

> Overwhelming experiences affect our innermost sensations and our relationship to our physical reality—the core of who we are. We have learned that trauma is not just an event that took place sometime in the past; it is also the imprint left by that experience on mind, brain, and body. This imprint has ongoing consequences for how the human organism manages to survive in the present.[105]

Van Der Kolk continues:

> Trauma results in a fundamental reorganization of the way mind and brain manage perceptions. For real change to take place, the body needs to learn that the danger has passed and to live in the reality of the present.[106]

Recovery from trauma is ongoing because the impact of trauma can continue to resonate throughout a survivor's life. Issues that were sufficiently resolved at one stage may be reawakened. Life creates many occasions that can return the earlier feelings of traumatic memories—marriages and divorces, births, or deaths in the family (particularly if the family member was involved in the abuse). Though the resolution of the trauma may never be complete because certain triggers may occur, there are ways to mitigate or bypass traumatic memories, feelings, or triggers that might occasionally arise.

## Four Tips for Healing Trauma[107]

1. Get moving.

Trauma disrupts your body's natural equilibrium, freezing you in a state of hyperarousal and fear. Exercise and movement can actually help repair your nervous system, and it can help burn off adrenaline and release endorphins.

2. Don't isolate yourself.

Following a trauma, you may want to withdraw from others, but isolation only makes things worse. Since connecting with others face-to-face will help you heal, make an effort to maintain your relationships and avoid spending too much time alone.

3. Self-regulate your nervous system.

No matter how agitated, anxious, or out of control you feel, it's important to know that you can change your arousal system and calm yourself. It will help relieve the anxiety associated with trauma, and it will also engender a greater sense of control.

4. Take care of your health.

Having a healthy body can increase your ability to cope with the stress of trauma. Get plenty of sleep. Avoid alcohol and drugs. Eat a well-balanced diet.

## Children and Trauma

Part of healing for children involves understanding toxic stress. According to pediatrician Dr. Dorothy Novick:

> Toxic stress—stress that is severe, unmanageable, and occurs in the absence of appropriate support—leads to physiological changes that permanently alter the architecture of the developing brain and other organ systems.[108]

The Centers for Disease Control and Prevention now implicate toxic childhood stress as a significant risk factor for a long list of cognitive, behavioral, psychological, and medical disorders—as well as for early death. To prevent and mitigate these effects, the American Academy of Pediatrics has called for a "new pediatric paradigm to promote health and prevent disease," which is built around a foundation of trauma-informed care.[109]

By definition, trauma-informed care involves prevention, recognition, and response to trauma-related difficulties.

Experts agree that incorporating an awareness of trauma into medical care requires a system-wide approach. As the front line in this new paradigm, pediatricians are conducting more screening to identify trauma in children.[110]

My work in therapy revealed many secrets and made many thoughts and feelings that were hidden in my subconscious, conscious. Dealing with trauma in my therapy was not easy, and it took an enormous amount of courage in my work with Jerry to face reality and release the shame I had been holding within me for more than forty years.

## Conclusion

It is very common for someone to experience trauma after a terrible or life-threatening event and suffer unpredictable emotions, flashbacks, negative changes in beliefs and feelings, and strained relationships.

Although the instigating event of the trauma may overpower either a child's or an adult's coping resources that are available at the time, it is still possible to develop healthy ways of coping with trauma and diminishing its effects.

## Chapter 9

# Breaking the Silence

*I have learned now that while those who speak about one's miseries usually hurt, those who keep silence hurt more.*

—C. S. Lewis

Disclosure of sexual abuse is often a process and not a single event. Youth who are coping with sexual violence sometimes act in ways that seem inconsistent with adult expectations of victims. The disclosure process may involve the victim revealing bits of information, not always in chronological order, and not always to the same individual.[111] Research confirms that many children do not disclose sexual abuse immediately after the abuse occurs. In fact, many children do not disclose the abuse for years, if they disclose it at all. And, as previously noted, many adult survivors of childhood sexual abuse have never disclosed their abuse to anyone.[112]

Two types of disclosure are accidental and purposeful. Accidental disclosures happen when the survivor conveys information to someone when it was not their intention to disclose the abuse. An example would be one friend telling another friend at school about an abusive incident and a teacher or other adult hearing this information. Another example would be a child undergoing a physical examination and the doctor noticing bruising or unusual redness around the anus and asking about it. Purposeful disclosures are when a survivor plans to convey the information of what happened to them, like telling a parent afterward. Purposeful disclosures have more positive outcomes overall because of a sense of empowerment and because they feel they were heard, if the person receiving the disclosure acts appropriately.[113]

My disclosure wasn't to a friend, family member, or coworker. Like many other survivors, my disclosure was accidental. As we have noted before, it happened during a dialogue with my therapist when we were discussing my childhood. I didn't plan on telling my therapist about the incidents of childhood sexual abuse. In fact, I didn't know it was sexual abuse.

According to research by national childhood sex prevention organization Darkness to Light, *disclosing* abuse refers to communicating an abusive experience to friends, family, or the authorities. *Divulging* abuse refers to communicating an abusive experience to researchers. There are many survivors to whom the first person they ever tell about an earlier childhood sexual abuse incident is a researcher collecting statistics.[114]

Disclosing your abuse to anyone can be difficult. One aspect of my numerous personal internal dialogues during my ongoing healing consisted of rereading the chapter "Seven Things You Should Never Say" in Marilyn Van Derbur's *Miss America by Day*.

1. "Did he rape you?"
2. "You need to forgive."
3. "Why didn't you tell me?"
4. "Why didn't you say no? Why didn't you cry out?"
5. "Why are you talking about this now? This happened decades ago. Let it go. Move on."
6. "We think it would be better if you didn't discuss this with anyone else."
7. "Why did you do this to your/our family?"[115]

Her words were important to me because the topics helped my understanding of what I was feeling and aided me in getting out of my unhelpful, negative self-judgment.

We do not have to bury our pasts in order to be fulfilled in our futures. Disclosure is highly personal, but breaking the silence is a key step to recovery.

## Low Disclosure Rates

Low disclosure rates are a defining factor in the issue of child sexual abuse. Low disclosure rates are a significant part of the problem that practitioners face when working to prevent or intervene in child sexual abuse.

There are a number of ways that low disclosure rates complicate the problem of child sexual abuse:

1. Low disclosure rates skew the number of reports and confirmed cases of child sexual abuse, minimizing the problem of child sexual abuse in the public's eyes.

2. Low disclosure rates are a variable that makes it difficult for researchers and practitioners to determine whether rates of abuse are increasing or decreasing.
3. If disclosure rates increase, it appears that child sexual abuse rates are increasing, when the opposite may be true.[116]

## Children and Disclosure

There is overwhelming evidence that when children do disclose, they disclose to a friend. Numerous studies have highlighted the role of peers as confidantes, particularly for adolescents.[117] While it may be true that children, especially older children, disclose to a friend or peer, with education and early communication, maybe this trend will evolve and more children will tell their parents when it happens—instead of someone else years later.

As we have noted, the children who do disclose to their parents often disclose to their mothers, especially when the abuser was not a family member.[118] Educators make up a majority of the professional reports of child abuse categorized as causing harm to the child.[119]

## Not Disclosing Abuse

Children who do not disclose immediately after the abuse have more major depressive episodes and delinquency in the future, and children who were victimized by family members have far more negative consequences if they delay disclosure.[120] These include symptoms of posttraumatic stress, negativity in childhood, and self-blame.[121] Prompt disclosure buffers the impact of severe abuse. It also makes it less likely that there will be additional abuse.[122]

Children who are abused by a family member are less likely to disclose and more likely to delay disclosure than those abused by someone outside the family,[123] and young children are less likely to disclose abuse.[124]

Females disclose more often than males, but females often resist disclosure because they feel responsible for the abuse, and they fear not being believed. Males are often reluctant to disclose that they have been sexually abused because they fear being labeled as a homosexual or as a victim.[125] Some males, especially adolescents who were abused by older females, believe the abuse speaks to their "masculinity and virility" and therefore don't think their sexual encounters with an older female constitute abuse.

## Why Telling Is Transformative

In *The Courage to Heal*, Ellen Bass and Laura Davis detail why disclosing sexual abuse can be helpful:

- You move through the guilt and secrecy that keep you isolated.
- You move through denial and acknowledge the truth of your abuse.
- You make it possible to get understanding and help.
- You get more in touch with your feelings.
- You get a chance to see your experience [and yourself] through the compassionate eyes of a supporter.

- You make space in relationships for the kind of intimacy that comes from honesty.
- You establish yourself as a person in the present who is dealing with the abuse in [their] past.
- You join a courageous community of [survivors] who are no longer willing to suffer in silence.
- You help end child sexual abuse by breaking the silence in which it thrives.
- You reclaim your voice.
- You become a model for other survivors.
- You [eventually] feel proud and strong.[126]

## Factors Encouraging Children to Disclose Abuse

Recent research has highlighted the need for children to be asked direct questions to facilitate their disclosure. Directly asking a child if they have been sexually abused can increase disclosure.[127]

Children are particularly susceptible to leading questions. Studies have shown that children are very attuned to taking cues from adults and tailoring their answers based on the way questions are worded.[128]

Questioners must use caution when asking leading questions. Examples of leading questions might be: Did your uncle touch you in a place you didn't want him to? Did that older boy make you do something you didn't want to do?

Some of the optimal conditions for disclosure include being directly asked about experiences of abuse; having access to someone who will listen, believe, and respond appropriately; having knowledge and language about what constitutes abuse and how to access help; having a sense of control over the process of disclosure both in terms of anonymity (not being identified until they are ready for this) and confidentiality (the right to control who knows); and effective responses by adults both in informal and formal contexts.[129]

In hindsight, I did not have this knowledge prior to the many years of my healing process. Even though I didn't have this information, my personal experience was representative of such optimal conditions for disclosure during therapy.

## Inconsistencies and Recanting

There is evidence that recantations and inconsistencies are common in child disclosures. Recanting happens when a child changes their story and suddenly denies that abuse happened. Inconsistencies happen when the events in a child's story are altered or remembered differently from the last time the child told their story.

Inconsistencies and recantations in children's reports may be due to reluctance rather than a false allegation. A child sexual abuse victim is more likely to recant or have inconsistencies in their story when a familiar person perpetrates abuse, especially if it's within the family.[130] Recantation often happens because of adult pressure or if the child sees consequences for their disclosure, such as the abuser being removed from the children's environment or jailed.

According to the childhood sexual prevention organization River Bridge Resource Center:

> Disclosing abuse is incredibly difficult for children. Recanting an allegation of abuse is not rare and is often affected by a child's vulnerability to adult and family influences (extending beyond caregivers i.e. grandparents, aunts, uncles, cousins). In all child abuse cases, it is estimated that children recant their stories about one-fifth of the time. Later in life, virtually all of those children who are now adults reaffirm the earlier childhood abuse.[131]

The decision to disclose your history as a survivor of childhood sexual abuse can be a confusing and difficult one. According to WINGS Foundation:

> It is a decision that we must continually make with each new person and in each new circumstance that we encounter. Because there is no right answer to this question or one right way to disclose this information, having some reference points of things to consider can make disclosures easier when faced with that decision.[132]

WINGS Foundation offers guidance when we are considering telling someone about our history of sexual abuse. They suggest the following things for us to consider before we disclose:

1. Are we disclosing this information at the right time in our lives?
2. Are we disclosing this information to the right person?

3. Are we disclosing this information for the right reason?
4. Are we disclosing this information in the right context?
5. Are we disclosing this information with enough support and resources in our life to handle any type of response?[133]

If any of the answers are, "I don't know" or "I'm unsure," talking about this with a therapist, support group, or trained professional from a children's advocacy center might help you move forward in determining whether or not it is the time to disclose an early childhood trauma.

While the recent #MeToo campaign has been a valuable tool for many, at times the immense movement has also had other effects, such as stirring up old triggers that one might not yet be prepared or ready to share. Linda Curran, a clinical psychologist and author of *Trauma Competency: A Clinician's Guide*, cautions survivors of childhood sexual abuse:

> Making your history public should only be done when you feel resourced enough to tolerate the effects of the disclosure. It's not heroic: it can be re-traumatizing or relieving, or it can be the beginning of therapy.[134]

For many survivors, their history of sexual abuse has been shielded in secrecy and shame for many years, sometimes even decades, like in my case. It is a burden that they have carried in silence or perhaps only shared with a few other people. But releasing the secret can help release the shame.[135]

## *Chapter 10*
## Triggers and Flashbacks

> *Triggers are like little psychic explosions that crash through avoidance and bring the dissociated, avoided trauma suddenly, unexpectedly, back into consciousness.*
> —Carolyn Spring

A trigger in psychology is a stimulus such as a smell, sound, or sight that triggers feelings of trauma. A trigger is a reminder of this past trauma and can cause a person to feel overwhelming sadness, anxiety, or panic. It may also cause someone to have flashbacks, which are vivid—often negative—memories that may appear without warning. Flashbacks can cause someone to lose track of their surroundings and relive a traumatic event.[136]

### Triggers

To a large extent, triggers are side effects of the brain trying to repress the painful memory of trauma. They are events, thoughts, or any stimuli that trigger emotional recall of the abuse or uncomfortable features of the abuse that the unconscious brain is attempting to stifle. For example, noticing someone with a similar feature of the abuser, such as the shape of their face, can result in anxiety, depression, or even panic, with no realization that such responses are related to one's abuse.

Triggers often produce unconscious, nonsexual, confusing responses. If innocuous stimuli—a color, a sound, a smell, or a personal manner—have been unconsciously related to the abuse, then their presence can trigger negative emotional responses, which can even be incapacitating, with or without any memory of the actual trauma.

It is not uncommon for people to seek psychotherapy for symptoms that later are identified as triggers created by some wholly or partially repressed experience. Triggers may continue to set off unwanted emotional problems, even when they are understood to be associated with abuse.

Dealing with triggers is frequently a central goal for recovery from sexual abuse. As previously discussed, essentially all psychodynamic psychotherapy is directed toward making the unconscious conscious. People seek therapy when they have some handicapping symptom they don't understand. (Why can't I stop eating uncontrollably when I hate being overweight? Why can't I sleep, get things done, find a life partner, or hold down a job? Why do I have some unexplainable physical symptom?)

All of these symptoms are in some way defense mechanisms designed by the mind to avoid the very insights people need to gain relief from the symptoms. An overweight person may need to know that they really are fearful of sexuality and unconsciously render themselves unattractive by being heavy. The person who can't hold a job may need to trace their intolerance of any boss to realize they are still fighting a long-ago battle with an overly authoritarian parent. Like many psychological symptoms, triggers need to be understood as unconscious responses. When decoded, these insights can lead to real symptom relief.

Understanding the connection between the symptom and the causative event often promotes the end of the symptoms. The person may have an aha moment, and the symptom may then disappear.

## Insights

Insight is when a piece of information gives you the understanding of a specific cause and effect, and this leads you to comprehend the inner nature of things or understanding something intuitively.

When the source of the symptom is out of the unconscious, the rational conscious mind can deal with the problem. However, in some cases, intellectual insights have little or no effect on the symptom. If so, the treatment involves one of two basic approaches: the treatment is either directed toward *emotional insight* or toward a slow but steady decrease of the symptom through *intellectual insight.*

Someone is said to have intellectual, but not emotional, insight when they acknowledge that holding a particular belief is irrational, but they say they still do not believe, or cannot accept, that fact.[137]

Someone is said to have emotional insight when they

understand the emotional forces underlying any symptom.[138] Emotional insight is reached when the symptom or trigger loses all effectiveness, such as when an overweight patient gets over their fear of sexuality and can achieve normal weight, or the job destroyer no longer expects bosses to be as unreasonably authoritarian as their father and can deal with leadership sans the emotions that lead to losing a job.

When abuse sufferers realize their triggers are symptoms of their abuse, they either experience them just vanishing (emotional insight), or they need to know that it will take time and constant intellectual work to dissipate the effect of the trigger.

Abuse sufferers too often minimize their recovery when they have any negative response to triggers. This is a mistake. Recovery does not involve an absolute absence of triggering. Instead, those who are in recovery can learn how to indulge in the relief of knowing why the triggers exist and knowing that the triggers can dissipate with time and understanding; otherwise, they can learn ways of handling them so they are no longer a mysteriously handicapping force.

Multiple times over the years, Jerry discussed triggers as any stimuli that stimulate some form of remembrance, consciously or unconsciously, of a traumatic event. The stimuli can range from very direct (seeing or recalling the abuse perpetrator) to very subtle (a weather pattern that existed during the abuse). That recall can be a full, part, or distorted memory of the event, and the triggered recall may produce only the emotional pain connected to the event without any awareness or memory of its relationship to the trauma. In a very real sense, triggers can be a hidden gift since they offer clues to what has been rendered unconscious and needs to be made conscious.

I have experienced many physical symptoms from my early abuse. I've learned that there are numerous ways of being triggered, and everyone's response to that trigger is individual.

In my case, I have learned from therapy to be more curious than confused when I am triggered. I am now able to recognize when I am having a strong reaction. During the same season I experienced trauma as a young child—fall—I can experience trauma as an adult.

Television drug commercials typically first list the treatment advantages of the advertised drug, and then, by law, they must list the negative side effects that the drug can also produce. Just like most all treatment drugs, the brain's pain reduction treatments also involve some unwanted and handicapping negative side effects. The difference is that drug side effects do not educate about the pathology whereas triggers can.

My therapist described the following nonsexual abuse therapy story, which illustrates the importance of how the unconscious part of our brains works to protect us, but often at a price.

A former client was driven to seek therapy because of his obsession with thinking about death. He was totally unable to control his obsessive anxieties about death. The thoughts were significantly intrusive to his general functioning. He came to therapy with no idea why he was suffering from the obsession. Early in therapy, he disclosed the important fact that he was also plagued by a reoccurring nightmare.

He repeatedly dreamed of himself as a young boy hiding under his childhood home porch in dread fear of something unknown that was terrifying him. The dream always produced uncomfortable, anxious feelings that lasted long after he awakened.

In therapy, the exploration of his subconscious eventually revealed the source of his symptoms. He had an old, wizened grandmother who had died when he was about eight years old. Prior to her burial, her open coffin rested in the family living room. His parents harbored the belief that the boy needed to kiss his grandmother goodbye in her coffin. Frightened by this thought, he actually hid under his front porch in fear of that action. However, unfortunately, his parents eventually forced him out of hiding to carry out the terrifying act.

Over the years, his unconscious mind was involved in saving him from pain by repressing—not allowing him to remember—the horror of having to kiss his dead grandmother. The unhelpful side effect was that he developed a conscious fear of death, and the quality of his life was diminished.

## Cover Memories and Anniversary Reactions

The reoccurring under-porch nightmare he had is known as a *cover memory*, which is another form of a trigger. Many traumas are accompanied by cover memories that are related to the repressed memory but allow only emotional memories of the event. Such emotional memories cause confusing pain without knowing what causes them. Triggers are a form of such emotional memories. In the example above, therapy was successful in uncovering the forgotten event, allowing the man to work through it, with his conscious, more rational mind. His nightmares and handicapping preoccupations disappeared.

An increase in distress around the anniversary of a traumatic event is commonly known as an *anniversary reaction*, and it can range from feeling mildly upset for a day or two to a more extreme reaction in which an individual experiences significant psychiatric or medical symptoms.[139]

Anniversary reactions are another form of a trigger and may occur on the anniversary date or season of a traumatic experience or incident. Many people are capable of going into unexpected emotional distress and are puzzled by an anniversary reaction.

A good example of an anniversary reaction is how people react to the 9/11 date each year. Many people without any history of abuse have strong emotional reactions on this date, and they have vivid recollections when they recall that tragic day.

When we have anniversary reactions, it can be helpful to pause and ask ourselves specifically what is causing this feeling of trauma. What is really going on in life to trigger this response? Embracing the memories can be extremely painful—but also astoundingly therapeutic and useful.

Several rituals can help people get through specific anniversary reactions. For instance, it might be helpful to really think about what happened during a specific time and honor that situation by processing the memory further, like going to church on the anniversary of somebody's death.

For my entire life, I experienced an anniversary reaction,

but I didn't know what it was. I just knew that I really disliked the autumn season, and I ultimately named it my fall malaise. I am now able to identify triggers, I know I have done the work, and I continue to do the work. I can stop beating myself up about it because it can get me stuck and panicky.

Foregoing negative thoughts when I am experiencing the fall malaise and recognizing that those times were quite traumatic and unpleasant are normal anniversary responses. Now, I can deal with it and be grateful because I have an increased awareness. I remind myself that we often feel more than one emotion at the same time, which makes life richer.

## The Wind ... Oh, the Wind

During the process of writing this book, at times, I was fighting the fall malaise, just like I had fought it for many years. I wanted to believe the anxiety had consistently waned, but even as I consciously put my tools to work, I sometimes experienced being triggered by the fall wind. The fact remains that the wind sounds different in the fall to me.

With Jerry's help, I have been able to explore why I have always had a visceral, emotional response to autumn. The sight of fall colors, the first leaves turning gold—the smells of autumn, the brisk feel in the air, and the sounds of the wind—are signs that can combine to create immense negative feelings in me, even though I intellectually know I am being triggered.

Autumn can create a panic that comes with powerful emotions, just as there was panic about my childhood sexual abuse for so many years. My confusion, shame, and silence led to what I now know are really posttraumatic stress feelings that I can experience during the fall season. Learning to understand the difference between memories, what might be triggering them, and current life was monumental for me. The simple reminder that "this is now, and that was then" is a powerful tool.

As I was writing *Meet Carey Jones*, I found correspondence and therapy notes from exactly a year before. Notably, the information was the same song, a new verse of what autumn can bring for me. In every autumn since I gained intellectual awareness, I wholeheartedly anticipate that "this year will be different." I remember all the time, thoughts, and energy of my therapy. Why do I continue to experience similar symptoms again? The difference is that now I quickly go to a state of curiosity, awareness, and action. Sometimes the action mitigates the fall malaise. Sometimes, self-compassion is as far as I can go.

Through therapy, I have learned and gained important knowledge and validation that my childhood sexual abuse experiences caused grave consequences.

Dr. Bessel Van Der Kolk's *The Body Keeps the Score* states:

> When something terrifying happens, like seeing a child or a friend get hurt in an accident, we will retain an intense and largely accurate memory of the event for a long time.[140]

He also states:

> One of the ways the memory of helplessness is stored is as muscle tension or feelings of

disintegration in the affected body areas[141] ... when people are chronically angry or scared, constant muscle tension ultimately leads to spasms, back pain, migraine headaches, fibromyalgia, and other forms of chronic pain.[142]

In the midst of my healing journey, there were also times when I unintentionally numbed myself or dissociated. During those periods, it felt as if I was "rolling up my car window" so that I had a barrier between my feelings and myself.

Dr. Van Der Kolk states:

> Long after a traumatic experience is over, it may be reactivated at the slightest hint of danger and mobilize disturbed brain circuits and secrete massive amounts of stress hormones ... These posttraumatic reactions feel incomprehensible and overwhelming.[143]

Over the years, I have learned that the first step of awareness followed by one of a handful of coping mechanisms has proved effective—the whole mind, body, and spirit connection. Simple deep breaths, multiple forms of exercise, and prayer all work together. I learned that knowing the strategies our brains use to attempt to guard us against psychic pain is an important introduction to learning how triggers work and how to deal with them. I found many benefits from multiple forms of exercise.

Van Der Kolk explains why in *The Body Keeps the Score*:

> In yoga, you focus your attention on your breathing and on your sensations from moment to moment. You begin to notice the connection between your emotions and your body—perhaps how anxiety about doing a pose actually throws you off balance.[144]

As a survivor, I learned to insulate myself from the emotions and physical horrors of that trauma when triggered. For many years, I remained unable to express the feelings and thoughts about that time, even to myself. For me, it was a long, long journey inside myself until those emotions and feelings eventually came out full-blown years later.

## Flashbacks

According to WINGS Foundation, triggers refer to anything in the present that takes us back to acting like we are living in the past, and a "flashback" does the same thing.

A flashback is like a frozen piece of memory or loop of videotape that contains an intense memory of trauma. The memory often contains a vivid "reliving" of an experience that may include visual (sight), auditory (sound), olfactory (smell), taste, and tactile (touch) sensations. Many times, flashbacks do not have an actual sensory component. We may have the sense of panic, being trapped, or feeling powerless with no memory stimulating it.[145]

Flashbacks may be associated with certain kinds of triggers that remind us of the past traumatic experiences, but they may also seemingly come from nowhere. Many veterans report flashbacks as one of the symptoms of posttraumatic stress.

As WINGS Foundation notes, when flashbacks occur, it's important to remember that they are not real. Flashbacks feel real, and they can send us back to the original trauma.[146]

One of the best ways to manage flashbacks is to recognize them for what they are— pieces of unprocessed past trauma—and then relocate ourselves back to the present. Again, awareness is the first important step followed by the ability to be personally kind and gentle with ourselves.

Triggers and flashbacks can feel like your emotions are being hijacked. When I am triggered now, I have coping skills and understand intellectually what is happening. Then, I search my brain to come up with everything in my toolbox.

When I am overcome with emotional responses, I attempt many *distraction methods*, which are very good tools and coping mechanisms. Calling my mom or sister for a chat unrelated to my current emotions is an example.

Be patient. It takes time to heal. It takes time to learn appropriate ways of taking care of yourself and developing coping skills when you regress into the past. Find a competent therapist or support group or both. You do not have to do this process alone.

## Chapter 11

## Self-Care

> *When you recover or discover something that nourishes your soul and brings joy, care enough about yourself to make room for it in your life.*
>
> —Jean Shinoda Bolen

"Self-care is something that refuels us, rather than takes from us," says psychologist Agnes Wainman. "Self-care isn't a selfish act. It is about knowing what we need to do in order to take care of ourselves, and, by doing that, we are also able to take care of others."[147]

Self-care is any activity that we do deliberately in order to take care of our mental, emotional, and physical health. Although it's a simple concept, in theory, it's something we often overlook. Good self-care is the key to improved mood and reduced anxiety. It's also an essential foundation for a good relationship with yourself and others.[148]

Self-care is different for everyone. It is imperative to define what self-care is for you and make those activities part of your daily routine. First off, understand that you deserve self-care; we all do.

As part of self-care, it's critical to realize that facing, dealing with, and healing from sexual abuse is an intense process. It's difficult to "create a good drawing without some shadows." I do not know of anybody recovering from sexual abuse who has not experienced moments of regression during the recovery process. If the regression includes self-deprecation, remember that even such negative side effects can feed into personal growth. It is, however, possible to learn how to cope with the feelings of regression throughout life.

Awareness is fundamental to the process of recovery and self-care. At the very least, being aware can help immensely when one is triggered, and it can alleviate many unpleasant downward spirals altogether. Triggers happen in life. Part of self-care is learning how to mitigate those triggers.

Know that excessive and heavy emotions are absolutely normal. Authentically feeling intense emotions aids in healing. Try to embrace them, learn from them, and feel them. Although confronting demons is often emotional and painful, in the end, it is very rewarding and often precedes a breakthrough.

I now have the awareness that I want to make sure I'm not falling back into an old habit. I want to make the point that I am now always fighting to change that behavior whenever I am triggered. We can be aware and change our thoughts. We can be in control and direct the flow of emotions more than we sometimes realize.

Habits are formed through repetition, which is tricky because triggers and flashbacks resurrect aspects of the trauma;

it feels as if it is happening in the present time. We relive these patterns and repeat them until they become our default normal patterns. Our learned responses happen automatically.

Creating new behavior requires awareness. When we are triggered, we can practice changing to a new, healthier behavior. We create an unconscious link between situations that happen and our actions by doing that. We can replace the old behavior with new responses and a new default setting with time, practice, awareness, and work.

Part of my self-care when I am triggered involves taking the time to identify what is being stirred up inside emotionally and intellectually. Sometimes, simply the awareness of what is going on can be enough. Sometimes, awareness allows me to choose to do something that has proven to work in the past.

Embracing the memory instead of shunning it is powerful. I have learned that refusing to let circumstances automatically control me is a step toward living a more balanced life. This takes practice, but it is full of positivity. The progress all stems from awareness and having the courage to embrace the transition into new behaviors.

Taking care of ourselves properly is difficult for many of us. As a society, we tend to frown on people who put themselves first. As survivors, however, it is critical for us to learn how to respect ourselves and put ourselves first in order to heal. By taking care of ourselves, we learn that we are worthy of positive, loving attention rather than the abusive, unhealthy attention we have received in the past.[149]

It is important to respect, love, and be good to yourself. Listening to your inner child and satisfying them are important steps in honoring our own needs. The needs of our inner children are often no more than simple love and/or nurturing. For example, if your inner child wants to be nurtured, schedule time to do just that.[150]

It is our responsibility to meet our own needs, and it sometimes involves asking others for help. It is not the responsibility of others—even loved ones—to try to guess our needs. We have to be able to articulate what we want in order to gain what we need.[151]

As survivors of childhood sexual abuse, we are often at a loss as to how to identify our own needs. Recognizing the personal worthiness of nurturing, love, and respect provides a strong foundation to honor those needs. Being able to identify both positive and negative situations and removing any negativity will result in more self-respect and self-worth.[152]

The balance created by making time for yourself results in a more positive and nurturing environment in which to heal and continue growing.[153] Embracing yourself in the present moment is a joy. Being present without judgment can result in a mind-set shift regarding your entire personal perspective of self-worth and identity. For me, my goal is to stay in awareness and gently remind myself when I get off course.

In addition to personal awareness, it might be helpful to be mindful or aware of others in your inner circle—your family and friends—with the intention of not wanting to overwhelm them with your process. It is fiercely important to have your support systems in place during recovery.

Learn to honor yourself by admitting when you need others to help and then be strong enough to ask for it. Many people who have experienced trauma feel disconnected, withdrawn, and misunderstood, and they can find it difficult to connect with other people. However, isolation has very adverse consequences, and reaching out for help is our responsibility.

I have learned that overcoming isolation with a supportive family, group, individual therapy, or friends is extremely helpful, but it is possible only when others are let in on the experience—whether it is joy or pain. Support is there if you take the step to bridge that gap. The possibilities are numerous and include support groups, volunteering, reconnecting with old friends, or making new ones.

Sometimes, periods of isolation can be helpful. When I'm having an emotional reaction, I still find it most useful at times to remove myself from the company of others because being misunderstood can be even more exhausting. By accepting what is going on and knowing the long, hard work I have done, I have more likelihood of acknowledging, giving due recognition, and then moving forward.

## Self-Care Suggestions

I like the suggestions on self-care from WINGS Foundation, which begin with making a list of "self-soothing activities."

My list would include yoga, healthy eating, going for a run or a gentle walk, riding my horse with my husband, snowshoeing, spending quality time with people who nourish me, calling a friend just to chat, prayer, relaxation, taking a hot bath, reading a book, listening to my favorite music, alone time, therapy appointments, meditation or journaling while feeling self-compassion, and laughter, which can be very healing and self-soothing. Self-care also includes being able to say no.

Exercising in nature has absolutely been an important part of my healing journey and self-care. Hiking in the mountains, both in solitude and with others, has been an instrumental aspect of my personal healing. While hiking, my soul is nurtured, and I think clearly. The Japanese have a term for using nature to heal; *Shinrin-yoku* means forest bathing.

Eating well, planning ahead for meals, and eating mindfully what nourishes my body, mind, and spirit are also parts of my healing. For others, it may be playing or listening to music, reading, doing creative work, or playing games. Each of us needs to learn what is healing for ourselves, and, when we slump, engaging in those activities can make us feel better.

Although the topic of sleep seems basic, the importance of sleep cannot be minimized. Sleep hygiene has been part of therapy discussions and has proven insightful, helpful, and critical to healthy living. It has also played into the important success I have had in preventing middle-of-the-night mindless eating.

> *I love the person I've become because I fought to become her.*
> —Kaci Diane

Self-care involves making sure that you are safe now and knowing that you are safe. The intellectual thoughts may come long before the desirable emotions do, but that's okay. Be gentle with yourself when triggers happen. It's a process.

Like many survivors of childhood sexual abuse, I still sometimes suffer from physical effects when triggered. Gratefully, with awareness, I am now able to focus on self-compassion, which leads to a much healthier response for me. From experience, I know which steps have been helpful in the past for dealing with any anxiety that might be stirred. The ability to act productively with no self-judgment, acting more like an observer, is a success that helps prevent falling into a spiraling vortex.

I routinely stated that I felt like I was back at square one after I was triggered. It still amazes me how often I felt that way (emotional) when I knew otherwise (intellectual). Gratefully, I eventually learned to skip the vortex by gaining the emotional insights.

If I am not able to alleviate all of the symptoms, I can always lessen them. Breaking the pattern by using self-compassion and self-knowledge, while eliminating self-judgment, is a triumph. As discussed in chapter 10, learning to mitigate triggers by understanding the origin is part of my self-care.

When triggered, my cycle used to look like this: being triggered by some external event or person, denial of feeling sad, upset because I didn't feel worthy of having the emotions (even though they were a result of being sexually abused as a child), and feeling shame.

For many years, that negative self-judgment: "you shouldn't feel this way or that way," sometimes occurred after being triggered. When I was unable to climb out of the self-condemnation, my self-loathing mind-set became so absurd that it finally propelled me to be compassionate with myself: to that little child within, to the adult within, and to the soul within.

I continue to learn that I can be more compassionate in how I treat myself. When I'm successful, I become and feel more productive and much healthier.

Learning to treat myself like I would treat others has been important. I'm not always great at this one, but, when I am on that path, I am clearly healthier.

Until recently, I had kept my personal battles very private. Now, I often find myself thinking that if I have experienced these lifelong internal struggles because of childhood sexual abuse, there are others who have suffered equally or more intensely, and, often, with self-inflicted isolation. To share my experiences, I have written this book and the following newspaper editorial:

---

The Aspen Times | Monday, June 25, 2018 | **A15**

**COMMENTARY**

## Protect your child, thoughts from a sexual abuse survivor

*Christie Somes, Guest column*

I was sexually assaulted by an older neighbor boy when I was 4 and 3 years old. That is a challenging, difficult statement for most people to read, and even more challenging for me to write. But I am not alone.

Rarely a week goes by without a jarring newspaper headline detailing childhood sexual abuse: a coach, a schoolteacher, a church elder, a father. Childhood sexual abuse is a crime that is far more prevalent than most people believe because most children do not report if they are being abused.

"Childhood sexual abuse is one of the biggest public health problems children and adults will face in their lifetimes, causing the most serious array of short- and long-term consequences," said Jenny Stith, executive director of the WINGS Foundation in Denver.

While many children are taught to be aware of "stranger danger," the sad fact is that someone they know is almost always the abuser. About 90 percent of children who are sexually abused suffer that harm from family members, someone close to the family or one of their classmates in school.

"Many people live lives with serious post-traumatic stress symptoms including anger, shame, guilt and a decreased sense of self-worth," said mental health therapist Meghan Hurley, River Bridge Regional Center in Glenwood Springs. "And the sad fact is that if we can reach them when the abuse is going on or shortly after we can greatly help their lives and decrease their suffering going forward."

While the subject of childhood sexual abuse can be troubling to talk about, there is good news. The recent #MeToo and #TimesUp campaigns have made everyone more aware about the issue of sexual harassment, and multiple celebrities, both female and male, have disclosed that their sexual harm happened to them when they were children.

As more people tell their truth about their past trauma, and how it affected them over their lifetime, more survivors are encouraged to come forward and get the help with the long-term effects of that earlier trauma and how it has affected their behaviors and physiological changes in their body.

Recent increased media awareness also encourages more parents and teachers (the No. 1 profession that spots abuse) to look for ways in which they can best protect children.

These parents, teachers and caregivers look to organizations like Denver's Parenting Safe Children (who recently held a sold-out workshop in Carbondale) for information on what they can do to keep kids safe. Founder Feather Berkower teaches how knowledge can help protect your children. Children need to know about their bodies, the real names of intimate body parts instead of cute terms and what's appropriate after other people to see and touch. They need to learn this information from you rather than from an uninformed childhood friend or worse. Who do you want to teach your children about sex, you or an abuser?

In addition to general information about their anatomy, you also can greatly increase the safety of your children by creating appropriate body safety rules and making sure teachers, coaches, church leaders, babysitters and any adult or older child who comes into contact with your children know about these rules.

I recently interviewed a 14-year-old accomplished gymnast from the Denver-metro area with soaring aspirations. But over a period of months, her 40-year-old coach used attention, praise and other classic grooming techniques to draw her closer to him until he inappropriately touched her, and there was no longer any question about his real intentions. Fortunately, the girl's mother had gone through a Parenting Safe Children's workshop, and she quickly recognized what was going on. The coach was fired from the gym where he worked, but Denver police have not prosecuted him, and he is once again working with another set of young, impressionable girls.

While I suffered from an array of behaviors and physical consequences for more than 40 years because of my early sexual abuse, I was able to get help, support and make my life better. Others who have been sexually abused can do the same.

Going forward, the patchwork of laws across our country can be more uniformly enforced. Survivors of early trauma should be encouraged to seek help through therapy and support groups. And perpetrators or organizations should be held accountable no matter how many years have passed. Over 20 states in our country have laws that limit a survivor from seeking justice from their abuser.

For more information about childhood sexual abuse, getting help and learning how to best protect your child, contact River Bridge Regional Center in Glenwood Springs (www.riverbridgerc.org), WINGS Foundation in Denver (www.wingsfound.org) or Parenting Safe Children (parentingsafechildren.com) in Denver.

*Christie Somes is currently collaborating with Steve Alldredge on "Meet Carey Jones," a book about her healing process from childhood sexual abuse and the latest information on the issue and prevention. She can be reached at: woodycreekstories@gmail.com.*

Self-care isn't just another task to put on the back burner; it is a topic that requires persistence. It is essential to set aside time and make self-care a priority. I learned that taking care of myself created a cascading effect of being a better wife, mother, grandmother, daughter, sister, friend, and person. Self-care leads to self-love, self-awareness, self-development, self-improvement, self-trust, self-respect, and self-worth.

Self-care can also award us with several health benefits, including improving our immunity, increasing our positive thinking and mind-set, and making us less susceptible to stress and other emotional health issues.

## Chapter 12
## Therapy and Support Groups

> *The job of therapists is to help people acknowledge, experience and bear the reality of life—with all its pleasures and heartbreak ... The greatest sources of our suffering are the lies we tell ourselves ... people can never get better without knowing what they know and feeling what they feel.*
> —Bessel Van Der Kolk, *The Body Keeps the Score*

In my life, the process of therapy has been a gift. Therapy helped create a healthy mind-set, new habits, a new thought process, and, eventually, healthy transformations.

Therapy can take many avenues and serve many different needs, depending on an individual's situation. For some, therapy may be aimed at a specific subject for a few weeks, while others may seek therapy for months or even years. With the right therapist or the right therapy group, the process can be extremely productive. As previously stated, therapy is digging out the unconscious with goals of making the unconscious conscious, growing in awareness, and looking at any resistance one might experience.

You make the decision to begin therapy for a variety of reasons. You might feel confused about something specific in life or have a more general feeling of a breaking point from the effects of being in emotional pain.

Both individual and group therapy offer tremendous benefits in their own right. They can both be enhanced by each other. Insights and growth can be gained from both group and individual therapy. Some individuals do better with just one type of therapy. Trust your intuition as to what combination suits you best. Your individual and/or group therapist may be able to offer you guidance on how to meet your particular needs.

## Therapists

The first step of beginning therapy is choosing a therapist. Many varied credentials can lead to confusion, but each accreditation merely indicates specific training. It is helpful to learn the differences between a psychiatrist, a psychologist, and a licensed therapist:

- A psychiatrist is a trained medical doctor who can prescribe medications. They spend much of their time with patients on medication management as a source of treatment.[154]
- A psychologist focuses extensively on psychotherapy and treating emotional and mental suffering in patients via behavioral intervention.
- A therapist is a licensed mental health professional who helps clients improve their lives, develop better

cognitive and emotional skills, reduce symptoms of mental illness, and cope with various challenges.[155]

Depending on one's personal needs, a multitude of approaches and training are available. When seeking a therapist, ask about their training, specializations, and types of treatment modalities they use in their therapy process.

In addition to determining which qualifications best suit your needs, trust your instincts to find a good personal fit. The mix of individual interpersonal and professional skills is unique to each person.

Below are some questions to ask as you select a therapist:

1. Is the therapist able to give sufficient explanations that you understand?
2. Do you feel trust from this therapist? Effective therapists have good interpersonal skills and are able to form alliances with patients/clients. Building a trusting relationship with a therapist is an integral aspect in the pursuit of awareness and insights through therapy.

During the first session with a therapist, it is common to be asked about the reason you're there or your *presenting problem*. You may have a specific reason, or it may be very general. It is not uncommon to begin talking about one issue only to have another more meaningful issue become the focus of therapy sessions.

It's common for a therapist to begin a session by asking you what you have on your mind that day. However, the direction may shift at any point. Sometimes, off-subject topics lead to profound insights. The relief a patient feels from solving one issue can lead to other, sometimes deeper, issues. Therapy can be a safe place where you can discuss and solve many different life issues.

During the course of therapy, you learn how to communicate with a therapist and build a relationship of trust and respect. An expectation that simply telling the therapist about your problems, and the therapist then solving or fixing your problems, is detrimental to the process. You need to expect that you will be required to deeply explore yourself, and you will not always be comfortable with your thoughts, feelings, and behaviors. With skilled guidance from a therapist, personal awareness can lead to insights into why certain problematic emotions or symptoms have occurred.

When my therapist did probe about my early childhood, the discussion could have been completely different if I hadn't trusted him. As my trust grew and the bond deepened with my therapist, I was able to reveal my childhood secret. Jerry had the knowledge and language of what constitutes abuse, and he was there to help me with the long-lasting consequences I had suffered but had never previously revealed.

Theoretically, you should be able to share any thought or feeling with a therapist. That is frequently hard to do. The ability to do so grows as the therapeutic relationship grows. But, when you find resistance talking about all or part of a feeling, belief, or happening, it's a good bet that it's an important subject for the therapeutic process. It is typical that such subjects are not faced the first time you experience them. With time, patience, and increased comfort in therapy, they can be approached. Resistance can signal an important element, whether repressed or otherwise.

Often, I felt stirred up after a therapy session. Although uncomfortable, I learned that discomfort signaled something important, and there were more insights to be gained from delving into the discomfort. Sometimes, choosing to heal some unknown parts of myself was painful because I felt so vulnerable. Now, I can look at those times as opportunities to conquer my fears. I have learned that vulnerability can ultimately lead to strength.

## Therapy Support Groups

A therapy support group is different from individual therapy. In a group experience, you easily recognize that you're not alone. Group therapy is a valuable experience where most people in the group can relate to others in ways never before experienced.

Support groups come in many varieties. Some are open with no limit on how long the group plans to meet, some are closed with specific time commitments, some are self-led with no organized leader, and some therapy support groups are directed and managed by knowledgeable leaders.

Most therapy support groups are formed with others experiencing a common illness or issue such as cancer, an addiction, or sexual abuse. Being with other people who are at different stages of the same basic problem has proven to be very helpful. Multiple studies have strongly proven the unique benefits of therapy in groups with participants who suffer from similar issues.

A client may do individual therapy first and then be prompted to explore a group experience. Other times, they may join a therapy support group and then decide to seek out individual therapy, often because another group member extols the benefits from working one-on-one on their own unique situation.

> *You gain strength, courage, and confidence by every experience in which you really stop to look fear in the face. You are able to say to yourself, "I lived through this horror. I can take the next thing that comes along." You must do the thing that you think you cannot do.*
>
> —Eleanor Roosevelt

## Group Experience

In addition to seeing my individual therapist, I eventually participated in a group experience specifically tailored for adult survivors of childhood sexual abuse.

Beginning to attend a group was a supportive and valuable experience, but it was not something that came naturally to me. In fact, I fought my therapist's suggestion to join a group for quite a while.

Involved in my resistance was fear of the unknown (anxiety) and intense reservations about sharing my story, which turned out to be a nonissue because it was not a demand of the support group to share anything at all. Many participants just listened and did not contribute any personal information for a long time or ever. How much is shared is each individual's decision with no pressure from the group.

In my therapy support group, I slowly let down my

shields of armor and any fear of judgment from others. I learned that staying below the radar was self-armor because it felt like a way of self-protecting. When we attach our self-worth to what others think, it can be dangerous because we are placing more importance on an external evaluation. Not relying too heavily on others' opinions of who you are, how worthy you are, or how you should best live your life is a goal for a healthy psychological state.

In *Be Fierce,* former Miss America Gretchen Carlson writes, "The pleasing syndrome is reflective of compliance."[156]

My desire to be a good girl became my handicapping need to be viewed as a good person by everyone until I was able to gain awareness and insight through therapy.

In my group support experience, I happily discovered the comfort of finding myself surrounded by others who deeply understood my issues and what I had gone through for more than forty years. Similar to myself, I found that many survivors had also suffered shame and did not tell others about their abuse experiences because they did not or still don't trust that others can fathom what they experienced. I had confirmation from others that childhood sexual abuse is not just the invasion of your body; it produces psychological symptoms that are devastating to various aspects of life.

Shortly after joining a sexual abuse support group, I developed the desire to join Speak Out! (www.wingsfound.org/event/speak-out/), an eight-week workshop that involved both writing and telling your individual story in a safe space. It turned out to be an important healing step for me. Speak Out! is a powerful process that invites you to be introspective, authentic, and vulnerable. The group dynamics were intriguing. Everyone in our group was totally different from one another, but we had a common thread of childhood sexual abuse. We immediately learned that the trust in the room was genuine, and the level in which we quickly became able to relate to complete strangers was astounding. At the end of the Speak Out! workshop, there was an opportunity to present your final story with an audience of other survivors and allies.

Both of my group experiences provided me with significant progress in my quest to heal from my sexual abuse. Both groups offered understanding and comfort as we shared our feelings regarding shame, dissociation, and other negative behaviors. To know you are far from unique in your responses to childhood sexual abuse dissipates huge blocks to healing.

As pre-support group adults, we may have long maintained the secrecy and our childhood silence, but the group experience provided a nonjudgmental space to share our truths. All members seemed instinctively supportive of each other with much mutual admiration, respect, and an intense connection.

I realize that this description is similar to my characterization and description of Carey Jones. When I was a child, Carey Jones was my support system.

My individual therapy, my group experience for survivors of childhood sexual abuse, and my work in Speak Out! were all unique experiences, but each form of therapy offered something different and something valuable.

As I reflect on my therapy experiences, I have learned that it is necessary to accept your personal stages with compassion and without self-deprecation. This is sometimes very difficult, but each stage is instructive.

I was closed off to many techniques used in therapy suggested by Jerry, such as free association, any testing (including Rorschach), psychodrama, and role-playing, and others. Now that I have a different knowledge and experience base, I am more open to exploring therapeutic methods for their potential help. What was I afraid of? Was it a fear of finding out that I was truly bad and unlovable? Everyone has a process they must go through for healing. Jerry patiently and skillfully helped me gain insights at the pace and with the techniques that my capabilities allowed at the time.

The emotions I felt during all my years of therapy were directly related to my own sense of self. Eventually, I realized that my closed demeanor was completely dependent on how unworthy or unlovable I was feeling.

It takes work and courage to confront the many disguises of deep insecurities. Learning how to be grateful for the tough times is another sign of growth. I have so much for which to be thankful, and a great deal of thankfulness is due to my therapy process and the additional work with the childhood sexual abuse support group and Speak Out!

# Part IV

*Practical Suggestions for Parents, Caregivers, and Educators*

*Chapter 13*

# For Parents, Educators, and Caregivers

*The way we talk to our children becomes their inner voice.*
—Peggy O'Mara

According to leading experts in the field, like Feather Berkower, LCSW, of Parenting Safe Children, as well as the national organization Darkness to Light, many incidents of childhood sexual abuse can be prevented. For parents, relatives, teachers, and anyone else who cares about children, you can learn how to protect children from sexual abuse by taking the burden off of kids to protect themselves.[157] All can take an active role in helping to protect children.

Lorna Littner LMSW, a New York-based human sexuality educator, explains why it is a group effort:

> I would suggest that the process of prevention education starts with the willingness and ability of parents and primary caretakers to talk with children under their care about sexuality.

Conversations that begin when a child starts asking questions or expressing curiosity most comfortably set the stage for a more targeted discussion of the issue of abuse as well as many other "difficult" topics. I am therefore suggesting that these early interactions emphasize the positive, life-affirming, and natural aspects of sexuality. These conversations normalize talking about sexuality and communicate to the child that it is okay to talk with parents about it. The additional benefit is that it provides a platform for parents to begin sharing their own cultural, ethical, and moral beliefs with their children.

How parents or other caretakers handle a survivor's sexual abuse when it occurs impacts the long-term effects of the abuse. If the child's abuse is discovered, or they disclose the abuse at an early age, they can get treatment at one of the 850 children or family advocacy centers that are now available across the United States. They can also get information and help from the many local wellness and mental health organizations that are now trained in working with sexually abused children and their families.

## Five Critical Skills

The earlier parents and caregivers talk to children about sexual assault and body safety, the better chance they stand to create lifelong awareness and prevention of childhood sexual assault. However, preventing childhood sexual assault takes more than educating children; it also takes teaching parents, caregivers, and entire communities about the issue of childhood sexual abuse, potential signs of sexual abuse, and how to have honest developmentally appropriate conversations with their children from the earliest ages.

This chapter discusses five critical skills my therapist suggests for parents, educators, and caregivers. It is our belief that many childhood sexual abuse incidents can be avoided, and the remaining incidents of abuse can be rendered much less severe if these five skills become part of your child's life.

## 1. Explaining Sexually Inappropriate Behaviors

Children should be equipped to recognize inappropriate behavior, and parents need to know how to explain, from a very young age, what behaviors are sexually inappropriate without frightening them.

Discussing sexuality with young children can be extremely difficult for many parents because of their past experiences with sexual issues and cultural or religious beliefs. We need to have open and honest communication about sexuality with children in order to build honest communication with them and increase their knowledge and protection when parents are not around.

The more a child knows about normal sexuality, the more likely they will realize when someone is being inappropriate with them—and the more likely they will have the skills to fend them off and report them. Adults are often uncomfortable talking about sex and consciously or unconsciously convey that sexual activity and private parts shouldn't be talked about. This contributes to children's shame and reluctance to disclose when something sexual has happened to them.

Lorna Littner, LMSW, offers the following natural behaviors for children of different ages:

## Birth to Three Years

Children are learning patterns of love, approval, and affection through bonding and touch intimacy. They often do not differentiate genitals from the rest of their bodies. The quality of their relationships is based on their observation/interaction with other family members. It is common for boys to have five to forty penile erections a day and for girls to lubricate shortly after birth.

## Eighteen Months to Three Years

Children discover their own bodies; they explore genitals and other body parts. It is common for them to touch or rub their genitals against their cribs or a toy that feels good. Being able to effectively explain inappropriate sexual behaviors or any aspect of sexuality to children involves using correct language with them from no later than age three.

## Three Years to Six Years

Parents and caregivers should incorporate into their language skills the proper names for their sexual organs, including words like *penis, vagina, anus,* and *breast.* During these ages, children begin to identify as boys and girls. They have an increased interest in their bodies, and masturbation and self-pleasuring are common. They may use sex words without understanding their meanings or play sex games with a childlike nonerotic perspective.

When age appropriate (ages four to eight), they should be taught the meanings for sexual behaviors, such as fondling, flashing, and masturbation. And, children should learn from their parents street names for the genitalia, and the exact meaning of sexual acts, including words like *tit*, *dick*, or *doin' it*.

## Seven Years to Twelve Years

During these ages, children's sexual experimentation increases, and curiosity about their bodies can lead to looking at pictures, masturbation, or having a crush on another person. They can also be concerned about the lack of physical changes in their bodies associated with puberty. Girls begin to menstruate.

## Thirteen Years Plus

During these ages, it is common to have an increased concern about physical appearance. Boys usually have their first ejaculation in the early part of this stage, and one-quarter of boys will experience their first ejaculation as a nocturnal emission (wet dream). Children begin to experiment with "adult" behaviors like alcohol and drug use. In the United States, more then 50 percent of girls will have intercourse by seventeen, and 50 percent of boys will have intercourse by sixteen and a half.

## 2. Talking to Children about Sex

"Children need to learn the correct names for their genitals," advises Lorna Littner.

> By avoiding calling a penis a penis, and a vagina a vagina, we unintentionally communicate that these are words that should not be spoken. We give power to the unspoken words. By the time a child is three or four, discussion about specifics can begin. These should be realistic and factual. Warning children about "stranger danger" is necessary, but not adequate, and it doesn't reflect the fact that people in their immediate or extended social network abuse most children ... When parents speak with their children using the correct words for all body parts, including the genitalia, they are building a crucial comfort level and normalizing discussions between themselves and their children about sexuality.

Talking and explaining about natural sexual activities should be done often and regularly. The classic approach of sitting down one time to talk to children about the birds and bees is exactly the wrong approach for educating children about sex. Typically, these discussions occur when children are preteens, and by that stage, they have already amassed much information regarding sexuality, much of it incorrect.

Some questions for parents to ask children include: What are the names and where are your private parts that others should not touch, have you show, ask you to touch, or look at theirs? What would you do if someone did something that was sexually inappropriate? Who would you tell if an inappropriate sexual event happened? After the child answers, the parent should praise correct answers and amplify or do more teaching for incomplete answers.

An essential part of all these discussions should include the fact that normal sexuality is natural, fine, and wonderful. Children should know that it is okay to have sexual feelings and that it is natural to explore your own body. The talk might include concrete examples of behaviors that are acceptable in public and those that aren't. For instance, they shouldn't "play with themselves" in public—just as they shouldn't pick their nose.

As children get older, it's normal for them to have sexuality-related discussions that include whether it's okay for them to be curious, feel sexual thoughts, or make out when they are at an appropriate age. This is going to be different for each parent, depending upon cultural and social context and religious beliefs.

Another opportunity to educate children is to bring up and discuss news events concerning sexual abuse, emphasizing how the children who were abused handled it. These discussions provide opportunities to teach children that keeping secrets, feeling helpless, or feeling guilty are natural responses and emotions.

They should also learn that when something inappropriate happens, the right response is to tell a parent, teacher, friend, relative, or the police as soon as possible. If the person they tell doesn't help them, they should keep telling other adults until someone does something about what is happening to them. This can be followed up with discussing why some victims don't report sexual abuse.

Educating children about what to do if someone touches them inappropriately or performs any other sexual act involving them is an important discussion to have with children. They need to know how to respond, and they need to know that these incidents should never be kept secret. They need to know that they are not at fault. Children should know how perpetrators try to keep what they do a secret and that they sometimes use threats or try to make the children feel guilty and responsible for what happened.

In *Off Limits,* Wurtele and Berkower counsel parents on the difference between secrets and surprises:

> Instead of keeping secrets, parents can teach their children that it's okay to keep surprises. Surprises are things that, after a while, you tell someone about, and it makes that person happy. But secrets are things people might tell you to keep to yourself and never tell anyone about. Secrets are never told, but surprises are most fun when they are told![158]

One way to gauge whether you are doing a good job with establishing good sexual communication with your children is when they feel able to come to you with questions, stories, comments, or concerns about sexuality. The child who feels comfortable asking natural questions about sex and sexual acts is prepared to better deal with sexuality and all of its complexities.

## 3. Establishing Relationships with Comfortable Communication

Parents need to establish relationships with their children so that children will comfortably share with them things that bother or confuse them. Children should be able to report to their parents without shame or fear about sexual matters.

The way to have an open communication relationship with your child is *not* to just say, "You can talk to me about anything." Almost every parent says that, and almost every child learns that it is not true. Children learn that keeping certain secrets from their parents keeps them from being punished or "bad," "stupid," or "an embarrassment."

How can parents maximize the chances that their children will share with them the more important issues in their lives? Parents can begin with the realization that everyone—children and adults—has a right to a certain degree of privacy. It would be terrible if others could read our minds all the time.

Parents need to remember that it is natural for children to not tell them everything. Instead, they are aiming for their children to see them as great sources of information and comfort, while, at the same time, respecting their right to certain privacies. Parents should allow and approve of each child to have some space (a drawer, a diary, a backpack) that they know will not be investigated by their parents or anyone (including siblings) unless given permission or behavior warrants it.

Trust between parents and a child begins at birth. Nurturing the child forms a bond. Parents continue to build trust through all stages of development, including when children begin making childlike mistakes such as breaking or losing something.

Parental correction of those mistakes needs to be done so that it does not negatively affect the child's self-concept. For example, neglecting to brush their teeth or forgetting to flush or losing their glasses for the umpteenth time should be thought of as a loving, teaching opportunity instead of an opportunity to berate or punish. Rather than punishments for poorly labeled "bad" behaviors, behavioral changes are best implemented with some kind of reward for "good" behaviors.

You can force behavioral changes with punishment, but the side effect weakens your child's honest relationship with you, and that is a much too precious price to pay. Children need to know that they are making "good" choices versus "bad" choices, instead of someone being "good" boys and girls versus "bad" boys and girls.

One extremely effective method that allows for children to share their "mistakes" with their parents is to have their parents admit to their own thoughtless or dangerous mistakes. It is a very effective parental practice to regularly volunteer and admit to the mistakes they have made. If parents can laugh with their children about the stupid things they have done, then children will understand that mistakes are not proof of inadequacy. Similarly, parents who share with children their confusions about issues teach children that it's all right to not know everything about all subjects. It's okay to let a child know that it takes more expertise or experience than you have to fix the car, repair the plumbing, or figure out your taxes. Too many parents attempt to have their children think of them as all-knowing, all-powerful, and mistake-proof.

When parents present themselves as mistake-proof, it makes the child feel less worthy by comparison. Parents who, even inadvertently, foster a poor self-concept in their children are providing them with a terrible handicap.

To raise children who trust you with their problems or concerns, parents need to interact with them as imperfect, nonthreatening sources of comfort and help. If parents would think of each interaction with their child as an opportunity to raise the child's self-concept and trust in them, then children will more often seek them out with their confusions or problems.

This does not mean that parents abdicate their responsibility for teaching and disciplining their children. It does mean that such responsibilities should be carried out with awareness of the effect they are having on the child's self-concept and view of their parents as confidantes.

## 4. Recognizing Obvious and Subtle Cues for Concerns

Parents need to learn to recognize both obvious and subtle cues from their children that suggest concerns, psychological pains, fears, or anxieties. Using effective communication methods that they have previously established allows parents to discover negative events in a child's life, such as troubling sexual events, without the child having to initiate communication.

The most obvious signs of children suffering from painful

life happenings that have not been discussed are unrelenting depressive or anxiety symptoms. These symptoms can be expressed through withdrawal, tears, sad faces, acting out, and hyperactive or hypoactive behaviors. Obvious symptoms become significant only when they last beyond the usual mood swings associated with normal childhood.

The subtler signs of psychological traumas with children younger than seven are generally exhibited through behavioral regressions to an earlier stage of development. A four- or five-year-old child might resurrect earlier toileting patterns such as soiling or bed-wetting, which he or she had long outgrown. They might display temper tantrums similar to their earlier years. In general, when young children's behaviors regress in any realm for a length of time, parents should be suspicious that the child is suffering some unaddressed problem.

With older children (preteen or teenage), the subtler signs of traumatic happenings that are not openly expressed frequently show up either as irritability beyond what is typical for those years or strong isolation behaviors, such as spending too much time preferring privacy and actively avoiding time with peers or family.

The most common sign of significant unaddressed problems for all ages involves sleep disorders. These symptoms can take the form of nightmares, prolonged sleeping, or insomnia. Children need more hours of sleep than adults. If they do not get it, it is a strong sign that something in their life is an ongoing struggle.

However, parents need not depend on particular behaviors as signaling problems they should address. Parental intuition that something is amiss with their child should be considered an unconscious call for help from the child. This raises the question of what a parent should do when they know or suspect their child is suffering from something of which they have not brought up with their parents.

Often, parents simply ask the child what is bothering them. If this is asked in a kind, caring way, this approach can work. On the other hand, angrily asking or demanding, "What's wrong with you?" is clearly not the way to go. If the child offers the typical response that "nothing is wrong" or some form of "get off my back," more complex techniques may be necessary.

Telling your children about your own life struggles, either in the present or during childhood, can be a bridge to useful communication. You can use examples:

- I remember being bullied or threatened when I was in the sixth grade. It was so bad that I didn't want to go to school.
- When Uncle Bill wanted me to hug him in a way that made me uncomfortable, I didn't know what to do.
- When I was growing up, I was really worried that I wouldn't know what to do on a date, and it made me feel foolish.

These conversations can help build a bond between you and your child—and help counteract any feelings of alienation they might be having.

Mel Littner, a very successful and respected sex educator, worked in the New York school system for decades. He would often meet with groups of schoolchildren he'd never met before to educate them about sexuality. The children would rarely ask questions that would allow him to give them important sexual information that was relevant to their particular personal concerns.

Mel was aware that offering general lectures about sexual matters was not nearly as meaningful as responding to personal questions the children had about their own current lives. To elicit meaningful personal questions and answers from the pupils, he stimulated the conversation by offering questions and answers that came from previous pupils. He called this teaching technique "stacking the deck." Hearing relevant questions from other adolescents encouraged the students to feel comfortable asking and discussing sexual matters with him, and it provided the children with illuminating useful information.

Mel collected the questions and answers from the hundreds of questions he and his wife, Lorna, had asked students over the years. Examples of the questions include: Why is my younger cousin having her periods (or developing breasts) when I'm not? How come my friend had intercourse but didn't get pregnant? If I've had a sexual thought about someone of my own sex, does that mean I'm gay?

Parents can use a similar technique by discussing personal experiences they may have never had in order to open up their children to discuss a current dilemma or discuss the experiences of a personal friend. Most humans share very similar sexual concerns during childhood and adolescence.

If parents are not able to somehow use the cues they see to open up their children to discussion and problem solving, they can elicit help for their children from other special adults. A teacher, clergyman, coach, neighbor, relative, or older sibling may have the kind of relationship with your child that would allow them to usefully delve into the suspected problem. There is also the option of seeking help from a child therapist.

## 5. Knowing How to Handle Sexual Abuse Revelation (also see next chapter)

When a sexual abuse event is made known to parents, or any other adult, they are responsible for two major actions: tending to the child and dealing with the perpetrator(s).

If a child reveals sexual abuse, parents can best spare children from ongoing psychological problems by offering the child support, comfort, and assurance of protection without generating any fears of parental or other retribution. If a formal report needs to be filed and the alleged perpetrator named, the child needs to trust that they will not be re-traumatized by the procedure.

The most important and absolute first response from parents or other adults to whom a child has revealed a sexual abuse problem is to praise the child for having the courage to convey whatever they were able to share without pressing for details beyond what the child voluntarily offers. It is also important to display loving, caring, protective attitudes toward the child before addressing how to deal with the situation and the offender.

Following the initial response to the child's revelation, there are important to-dos and not-to-dos. The most difficult not-to-do comes right at the beginning. It is important that you are not dominated or led into precipitous actions by the understandably very strong emotions you will experience when you first learn that someone has sexually abused your child. Emotions like rage, fury, and an impulsive feeling to strike out against the perpetrator may flood over you.

Resisting those justifiable revengeful urges can best be done when you are keenly aware that the first and most critical to-do is to psychologically tend to the child. The child needs immediate and convincing reassurances that they did the absolute right thing by telling someone what happened to them. They need to know that they are not guilty of anything, and that, while it is common, they do not need to be ashamed. Instead, they are heroic for having told an appropriate adult.

Parents and others should use their most thoughtful judgment in communicating these positive concepts to the child.

Using methods that will not upset the child, the next to-do is to convince them that you will absolutely be able to protect them and others from the perpetrator.

Parents have many options in getting help developing a good plan of action or getting questions answered about how to handle an incident of childhood sexual abuse. There are children's resource centers across the country, local social service agencies, and national hotlines that can assist you. You may wish to turn to a child psychologist and/or a knowledgeable attorney. Children's resource centers offer staffs that are specifically trained to deal with childhood sexual abuse. A psychologist can offer counsel for how to confront the perpetrator, while protecting and aiding the abused child. And an attorney can protect the child from legal agencies that could negatively impact the parents or the child.

The child should understand what is going on with words at their age level before you move through the process. The goal is to not re-traumatize the child with any methods that perpetuate fear or discomfort or require them to do something they are not emotionally prepared to do, such as having to be interviewed by legal authorities or anyone else with whom the child indicates they are not ready to talk. This may even include not discussing the incident with a family member who they love.

A child shouldn't be forced to provide details of abuse to the parent, and they often won't want to. However, a child should also be assured that they can share anything they choose to share with you.

Even if you feel the child could have done something earlier or better, reassure them that the way they handled the abuse was fine. The child—being so prone to guilt, anxiety, depression, and shame—needs to be comforted by feeling their parents approve of and completely understand how they responded.

Regardless of who the perpetrator is—another child, a family member, a coach, a stranger, or whomever—they need to first be stopped from inflicting any further abuse. When it comes to dealing with a sexual abuser, keep in mind that all situations need to be handled individually.

The most dangerous approach involves taking matters into your own hands. As parents, your justifiable, strong emotions and thoughts regarding the perpetrator disqualifies you from making rational, safe, or legal decisions regarding them. No vigilante actions should be considered. As difficult as it may be, the wisest response is to allow people with the appropriate expertise to deal with the perpetrator. They are equipped and motivated to provide you with information and solutions without endangering you or your child.

## Mandatory Reporting

According to Darkness to Light, mandatory reporter laws may be in place in your state, and they typically require people who work closely with children in their professions to alert police or the appropriate authorities about suspected abuse. Mandated reporters include teachers, health care personnel, mental health professionals, employees in youth-serving organizations, law enforcement, and other professions as required by law.

Many people assume that disclosure results in a report to the authorities. This is not true. Children are highly resistant to disclosing to the police, according to the staff of River Bridge, a children's resource center. Delayed disclosure is extremely common, which is counterintuitive for many people.

In some states, all adults are considered mandated reporters. This means you are legally responsible for reporting suspected or disclosed childhood sexual abuse.

If a child is in immediate danger, always call 911.

## Forensic Interviews

It is critical that any child who may have been a victim of sexual abuse participate in a forensic interview as soon as possible. Child advocacy centers are specifically equipped to facilitate these kinds of interviews.

A forensic interview is a specially designed interview for children who may have been victims of, or witnesses to, a crime. The goal of the forensic interview is to provide a safe and welcoming environment for a child to be able to provide a narrative explanation of what they saw, heard, and/or experienced without being traumatized in the process. Forensic interviewers are highly trained to facilitate these interviews to make the child feel comfortable. Utilizing open-ended questioning techniques ensures that the most accurate information possible is obtained from the child and that any information obtained from the interview comes from the child and not the interviewer.

Forensic interviews should take place in a child-friendly room that is free from distractions. They will be audio and video recorded to preserve the child's statements and demeanor. This will also prevent the child from having to be reinterviewed or having to repeat their story to a number of different people. Interviewers may be law enforcement officers or specially trained civilians who are hired due to their warmth, friendliness, and demonstrated ability to work with children.

It is important to insist that anyone questioning your child have previous trauma-informed training. If you question someone's skills who will be interacting with the child, insist that you and/or a qualified mental health expert be present during any interview with the child.

If the abuser is a family member or another child, reporting the abuse can be a very delicate matter if proper protocols are not followed. Parents and others must also consider the fact that the accused will almost certainly deny the allegation, leading to a he says, she says case, with the abused child having to face difficult interrogations.

With the help of legal professionals, you should be able to come up with a reasonable plan for how to best confront and deal with the offender. You need to feel confident you are not acting out of compelling emotions, and you need to be sure that the child will not be hurt in any way by this interaction.

## Assessing How Abuse Has Been Handled (also see next chapter)

If your child has been sexually abused, you need to be able to assess the success of dealing with your child. You need to be able to decide if your child requires further professional help and whether the community needs further safeguards against the perpetrator.

The effects of sexual abuse on a child cannot be cured in a week, a month, or a year. In some cases, such abuse causes psychological handicaps throughout life. These handicaps are typically not constant, but they can happen periodically, such as when they are activated by certain triggers.

Regardless of how well things are handled when a child initially reveals they have been abused, or how well the child appears to be after some amount of time, it is wise to be prepared to deal with various kinds of aftershocks long into adulthood.

Sexually abused children (and adults) can experience symptoms that are similar to veterans with combat-related posttraumatic stress disorders. They can struggle with flashbacks, associated-fear reactions, sleep disorders, and other symptoms, constantly or periodically, for months and years.

You and your child need to be able to recognize these symptoms and their origins and have some therapeutic way of dealing with them. A therapist or therapy group that is available on an as-needed basis is probably the most common way to deal with any reoccurring symptoms.

Some children and adults who have been sexually abused can also independently deal with the recognized aftereffects of sexual abuse through self-administered healing techniques involving such things as meditation, wilderness visits, yoga, or a spiritual-based activity, as we have previously noted. Myriad health-providing physical and psychological techniques have proven to be helpful to childhood sexual abuse survivors.

There are also self-destructive ways of escaping the pains of reoccurring sexual abuse symptoms, such as overusing licit or illicit drugs or alcohol or any addictive activity that is ultimately detrimental to your well-being. Finding a way out of the detrimental strategies for dealing with sex abuse aftermath typically requires professional help.

The major takeaway is that it is common for the negative symptoms from sexual abuse to reappear long after the original abuse has ended and its initial effects have been "handled." Being aware of these symptoms and managing the negative effects shows that you are on the road to recovery. Getting a child help early on in the process, soon after the abusive incident, will help mitigate any long-term effects of the abuse.

Uninformed outsiders may say or imply unfortunate, unhelpful, or even damaging things to victims of former sexual abuse, including: "Isn't it time you got past that?" Such wrongheaded statements can cause pain and guilt from survivors. It can make them inappropriately feel like they have been negligent or weak or purposely malingering when in fact the usual prognostic expectation is for some serious sexual abuse effects to remain active or dormant throughout the victim's life.

Besides making sure that your child is properly treated, the responsibility of parents is to learn how the abuser has been confronted and legally held responsible. If they are satisfied with what has happened, they have completed their duty. If they are not satisfied, they need to pursue all appropriate agencies—police, government child protection agencies, and other legal entities—until they are satisfied that all children, adolescents, and adults need not fear any further abuse from the offender.

The offender should expect lifelong consequences for their actions. Those legally found to be sexual predators will have to live with that legally permanent label and register with the local authorities wherever they live.

If parents are not satisfied by any of those agencies, there are a large number of public and private organizations that are devoted and skilled at helping citizens deal with all aspects of sexual abuse, including dealing with perpetrators. Some of these groups are listed at the end of this book or on the Meet Carey Jones website (www.meetcareyjones.com). There is no cure for pedophilia, and someone's assurance that "it won't happen again" is never enough, no matter who they are, including close family members.

## Internet Safety

The Internet provides an opportunity for children to learn, explore the world, and socialize with friends. However, in our modern age, the "stranger danger" that may be endangering your child may be online. Darkness to Light offers the following tips and guidance on keeping children safe in our digital age:

### General Tips and Guidance

Make sure your youth-serving organizations have and enforce communication policies that protect children. Teachers, instructors, and other youth workers should not be communicating privately with children. Instead, they should use group texts, messages, or other communications, and they should include parents.

Do not underestimate the level of sophistication that an abuser will use to approach your child. Pay attention to all downloaded apps and their capabilities—even ones that do not seem to be related to chats.

Smartphones and tablets have a location services feature that allows devices to broadcast their location to the users' apps and contacts. Ensure this feature is turned off to ensure your child's whereabouts remain private.

If you discover questionable communications from your child to an adult or other youth, remain calm. Be sure to talk to your child without accusation and with the goal of resolving the situation. It is essential that parents, teachers, and anyone who suspects sexual solicitations in any form report it. They should also report bullying or child pornography immediately to local law enforcement.[159]

## Pornography

Pornography is easily available or accessible to children on the Internet. Many children use pornography as "education" for learning about sexual activities. It is important for both boys and girls to know that pornography is staged and not realistic sexual behavior. Parents need to learn how to block pornography on their children's computers and in the homes of their children's friends or other places where the child may access it.[160] But even the most Internet-cautious parents should assume that their children will find and be exposed to pornography. This means you need to discuss with them all the facts, attitudes, and sexual activities that are so misleading about pornography. And teens should be taught that it is illegal to download pornographic images of underage children or to text or email those images to anyone else.

## For Younger Children

Using computers at a young age requires direct supervision and parental responsibility. Knowing which games, apps, and learning tools have communication and chat capabilities is an ongoing, necessary task in today's society. Always keep children's personal information off of any online profiles. Like any other developmental stage, it is important to discuss all aspects of using a computer with your children.

Candid, open communication between children and parents regarding computer usage, including positive and negative possibilities, demonstrates another example of an important conversation parents can and should have with their children.[161]

## For Preteen Children

Set reasonable time limits on computer, smartphone, and device use, and when possible, limit usage to common areas of the house where parents or caregivers are present. To protect children, set privacy settings to the highest levels. Talk to children about the apps and services they use and how they use them to communicate. Pay attention to games and gaming systems, which often have online communication capabilities. Chatting can be an enjoyable activity that accompanies digital fun and learning, but it requires oversight and parental involvement.

Monitor texts, messages, and other digital communication—and explain why this is a necessary step for protection. Abusers use sophisticated grooming tactics that may be above the children's level of understanding. By monitoring communication, you are in a better position to identify a situation if it does occur.

Talk to your children about topics like sexting and cyberbullying. Explain the potential long-term consequences of sending sexual messages and pictures. Tell children if they hear of this happening or if anyone sends them an inappropriate communication—no matter who it is—to tell you immediately.[162]

## For Teenagers

Talk to your teens about the dangers and permanence of communications sent digitally, including on social media and blogs. Explain that popular applications that claim to delete images and messages still retain them and those private messages and comments are actually public and can easily be shared. Periodically monitor device use, including emails, photos, messaging, and app usage. Make sure teens understand this is not to punish them but to protect them. Let your teens know they should come to you if they ever have questions about a communication or if anyone makes them feel uncomfortable. This involves having developed their trust that you will not respond in ways that might embarrass or punish them or their friends and that you will decide together how to handle the incident.[163]

## For All Ages

According to the FBI's *A Parent's Guide to Internet Safety,* make sure children know:

- Never chat with someone they do not know or arrange a face-to-face meeting with someone who contacts them through an app or online service—even if they claim to be another youth or a friend of a friend.

- Never give out identifying information such as name, home address, neighborhood, phone number, school information, or extracurricular organizations and activities.
- Never post public photos of themselves, send photos to someone they do not know, or send explicit/inappropriate photos to a friend or significant other.
- Never download pictures from someone they do not know because there is a chance they could be sexually explicit.
- Never respond to messages or posts that are suggestive, obscene, bullying, or harassing.[164]

## Five Steps to Protection

For parents, Darkness to Light offers *The Five Steps to Protecting Our Children*:

1. Learn the facts. The facts about child sexual abuse can be staggering, but they can help us understand the risks children face.
2. Minimize opportunity. If you eliminate opportunities for children to be in isolated, one-on-one situations, you can dramatically reduce the risk of abuse.
3. Talk about it. Children often keep abuse a secret, but talking openly about our bodies, sex, and boundaries can encourage children to share.
4. Recognize the signs. But don't expect obvious signs when a child is being abused.

5. React responsibly. Be prepared to react responsibly if a child discloses abuse to you or if you suspect or see that boundaries have been violated.[165]

Sexuality educators Mel and Lorna Littner offer two other suggestions:

1. Be prepared and proactive in initiating these teaching-learning transactions. If you have a partner, talk about what you both want to communicate so that you are on the same page and are giving the same uniform messages to the child.
2. Framing messages about sexuality or sexual abuse prevention in concrete, easily understandable, and non-frightening words that can easily be understood by all children, especially younger ones, can be harder than one thinks. If you are nervous or feel unsure about what to say and how to say it, practice communicating it. Think about how you can say things that are appropriate for the developmental stage or age of the child.

There are many different local and national trainings in preventing childhood sexual abuse around the country. A few of the national organizations that offer these trainings are listed in the appendix of this book.

## Chapter 14

# What To Do If Your Child Discloses They Have Been Sexually Abused

*Truth does not change according to our ability to stomach it.*
—Flannery O'Connor

Provide safety, love, and support. Let them know that it is okay to cry or to be mad or sad or frightened or confused. Make sure your child understands it is not his or her fault. Don't pressure your child to talk about things. Praise them for whatever they have revealed and let them know you (and others) will not be permitted to have them say anything they are not ready to talk about.[166]

### When a Child Discloses That They Have Been Abused

While one form of disclosure is telling someone else your story about the childhood sexual abuse that happened to you, another form of disclosure is having a child tell you what happened to him or her.

In *Helping Your Child Recover from Sexual Abuse*, Caren Adams and Jennifer Fay offer practical information on what to do and what to say to your child when they disclose to you they have been sexually abused. More than likely, they will only tell you this information after repeated, persistent questioning.

According to Adams and Fay, your first response to a child telling you that someone has done something bad and inappropriate to them is to say, "I believe you."[167]

Your first task is to find the facts and separate your natural reaction to the overwhelming bad news. Your child needs to know that you believe them and that you will support them. Children who have someone understanding and supporting them suffer fewer ill effects than do children without help. Your role as a parent is to support your child in recovery by providing reassurance, safety, and love. You must also make decisions about medical care, legal proceedings, and counseling. Children need reassurance that they didn't cause your anger, upset, and sadness.[168] A child might associate a parent's tears as being upset with the child rather than being in pain by what the child endured.

## How Do I Know My Child Is Telling the Truth?

This is a natural question for parents. Children rarely lie about sexual abuse. They are more likely to deny abuse has happened than to make it up. Children usually don't know enough to make up the abusive incidents they describe.

It is often easier to believe the abuse didn't occur than to believe that someone, especially someone you know and trust, really does sexually abuse children.[169]

## Finding Out Your Child Has Been Sexually Abused

Finding out that your child has been sexually abused can be a parent's worst nightmare. You may blame yourself for not protecting your child. You may be isolated because people believe the offender instead of you and your child. No parent can be everywhere at all times. Symptoms and signs can be hard to see. Very few children come right out and tell their parents.[170]

Fay and Adams also suggest a few don'ts:

> Don't restrict your child's play or other activities any more than you must for your own peace of mind. The child may see this as punishment. If your child wants to cling to you for a few days, don't be afraid to let her/him. Don't let your desire to make sense of what has happened lead you into probing questions about details of the abuse. Don't ask why they didn't say "no" or tell sooner because that can increase their feelings of guilt. Don't make any promises on what will happen to the offender, or promise that the child will never have to see the offender again. Don't urge your child to just forget it.[171]

## Helping the Child Before and After

Understand why children are afraid to tell. Some children are too young to understand. Some children who do not initially disclose abuse are ashamed to tell when it happens again. Children are afraid of disappointing their parents and disrupting the family. Children often love the abuser and don't want to get anyone in trouble or end the relationship.

Abusers often shame the child, point out that the child let it happen, or tell the child that their parents will be angry. The abuser is often manipulative and may try to confuse the child about what is right and wrong or tell them the abuse is a "game." The abuser sometimes threatens to harm the child or a family member.[172]

Understand how children communicate. Children who disclose sexual abuse often tell a trusted adult other than a parent. For this reason, training for people who work with children is especially important, and this is especially true when finding the right therapist for your child. Children may tell portions of what happened or pretend it happened to someone else to gauge adult reaction. Children will often shut down and refuse to tell more if you respond emotionally or negatively.[173]

I have previously noted that I did not tell anyone about or disclose my childhood sexual abuse that happened when I was four and five until I was in my midforties, which is a fairly common occurrence for survivors. As we have seen as a result of the recent #MeToo and #TimesUp campaigns, many women and men have not disclosed their childhood sexual abuse traumas until decades after it happened.

As statute of limitation laws are changed and adult

survivors are finally coming forward after years or decades of silence and filing lawsuits for past abuse against individuals, religious institutions, public and private schools, organizations, and others, the healing power of telling their stories will help many of them move forward with their lives.

## Things You Can Say to Help Your Child

As we noted in the previous chapter, it is important to let the child know they have done the right thing by telling you what happened.

1. You can tell them: I believe you. I love you, and we are going to get through this. None of this is your fault. I'm so glad I know about it now so you do not have to be alone. I'm so proud of you for telling. I'm sorry this happened to you. I will take care of you. I'm not sure what will happen next. Nothing about *you* made this happen. It has happened to other children too. You don't need to take care of me. I am upset—but not with you. I'm angry with the person who did this. I'm sad. You may see me cry. That's all right. I am not mad at you. I don't know why the person did this. They have a problem, they need help, and they need to face the consequences of what they did. Unfortunately, this happens to a lot of kids, and there are people who will help us get through this. You can still love someone but hate what they did to you.[174]

2. Protect your child by getting them away from the abuser as quickly as is feasible. After making sure the child feels safe, report the abuse to local authorities. If you are not sure who to contact, call the Childhelp National Child Abuse Hotline at 1.800.4.A.CHILD (1.800.422.4453, www.childhelp.org/get_help) or for immediate help, call 911.[175]
3. Keep your child informed about what will happen next, particularly with regard to legal actions. (For more information on helping abused children cope with the stress of dealing with the legal system, see the National Child Traumatic Stress Network's *Child Sexual Abuse: Coping with the Emotional Stress of the Legal System*, available on the web at: www.nctsn.org/resources/child-sexual-abuse-coping-emotional-stress-legal-system.
4. Consult your child's primary care physician or your local child abuse assessment center regarding possible follow-up medical care.
5. Call the Department of Human Services (DHS) office in the county in which your child lives or where the abuse occurred to report your concerns. The child needs to know about making such contacts so spend time explaining the call until the child understands the need for doing so.
    - https://www.d2l.org/get-help/reporting/making-a-report/
    - https://www.d2l.org/get-help/reporting/mandatory-reporting/

- https://www.d2l.org/get-help/reporting/protection-laws/

After finding out that your child has been sexually abused, know that they will need special help and services from a doctor with special training in responding to child victims of sexual assault and/or police officers who are specially trained to speak to children about sexual abuse and for counseling from a trained therapist who can provide objectivity and distance, allowing your child to work through issues that are too painful for you to tackle together.[176]

## Who Do I Call? Where Do I Go? Do I Need a Lawyer?

A lawyer who has expertise in dealing with social agencies may be one of the first people you call.

### Victim's Advocacy Attorneys

Victim's advocacy attorneys are specifically dedicated to legal representation of victims as they go through the court process.

The victim advocate is available to intercede on behalf of victims with family and friends, law enforcement officers, and prosecutors. Advocates become involved in a case after a police report is filed. Even if there is no suspect and no prosecution, the advocate is dedicated to responding to the needs of the victim.

## Child Advocacy Centers (CACs) and Family Advocacy Centers (FACs)

Depending on the state where you live, CACs or FACs will coordinate all the professionals (legal and social services) involved in a case. If you're unsure about whether to make an official report or just need support, contact a child advocacy center or a family advocacy center. They will help you evaluate your suspicions. To find one near you, contact the National Children's Alliance at www.nca-online.org or 1-800-239-9950.[177] If you have any questions or concerns that have not been addressed by a CAC or FAC, use a knowledgeable lawyer or victim's advocate to help you.

## Child Abuse Helplines

Helplines have staff specifically trained operators to deal with questions about suspected child sexual abuse. Call Darkness to Light's Helpline, 1-866-FOR-LIGHT, to be routed to resources in your own community or call the ChildHelp USA National Child Abuse Hotline, 1-800-4-A-CHILD.[178]

## Local Community Agencies

Look for local agencies, such as local hotlines, United Way offices, or rape crisis centers that can often help.

## Prevent Now

According to Darkness to Light, child sexual abuse affects more than just children and their families. It also affects entire communities. To address the issue and better protect children, adults in the community need to be proactive and join forces. Darkness to Light's *Prevent Now!* is a program that assists and supports communities in creating child sexual abuse prevention initiatives that increase awareness, education, prevention, and advocacy. *Prevent Now!* holds workshops that help individuals form groups of ten or more participants who are willing to learn more about childhood sexual abuse and how to prevent it.[179]

The goal is to have more adults and more communities have this type of knowledge and training so that all forms of childhood sexual abuse and issues, such as grooming, will be noticed and acted upon appropriately. If more adults recognize the signs of childhood sexual abuse and have established, trusted relationships with their children, which includes honest communication, abusers will be less likely to infiltrate that healthy, strong environment.

## Stewards of Children

Stewards of Children is an educational training program created by Darkness to Light (d2l.org) to increase knowledge, improve attitudes, and change child-protective behaviors. It is appropriate for any adult, and the training will teach you how to prevent, recognize, and react responsibly to any incident of child sexual abuse.

## Chapter 15

## Moving Forward

*You can't change the past, so change
something you can—the future!*
—Erin Merryn

It is a sad fact that sexual abuse is pervasive in our society. It should no longer be a secretive and shameful subject.

The completion of Meet Carey Jones has left me in awe as I look back at all that has transpired since I began writing this book. The many people, worldwide, who shared their stories in the #MeToo and #Times Up movements inspired me. The brave women of the US Olympic gymnastics team inspired me. The women who have given voice to the many instances of harassment in Hollywood and the entertainment industry inspired me. I have also been inspired by the many women and men who have raised their voices about long-term abuse in our places of worship, national organizations like the Boy Scouts, and the military.

As I was completing *Meet Carey Jones*, the state of New York implemented a new law that for one year removed the statute of limitations on filing a claim of sexual abuse. Not surprisingly, it is as if the floodgates were lifted as thousands of survivors reported past abusive situations.

It seems like there is much positive movement, which energizes me, but sometimes I am frustrated by the fact that childhood sexual abuse won't go away without our cumulative, consistent efforts.

As adults, we are responsible for teaching children what is and isn't appropriate, teaching them that they are safe to talk about the subject, and keeping them free from dark, toxic secrets.

Adults are responsible for teaching children about their bodies, teaching them that their bodies are theirs, and for being alert for when grooming might be going on. Some people still have an attached belief that predators are all strangers or obvious "bad people." Sometimes, the fact still doesn't equate in our minds that a predator could be a beloved or the least expected person in our lives. It is adults' responsibility to dismiss those people from our children's lives in order to protect them—even when it is no minor task.

When prevention happens instead of abuse, a world of trauma is avoided. This takes education, alertness, and openness with parents, teachers, caretakers, and medical doctors, including pediatricians, family doctors, and OB/GYNs (to name a few). When trauma does occur, it takes all of these same people and professionals to make an impact on recovery. Otherwise, the long-term impact of a disastrous response can result in increasing the cycle of trauma.

When a survivor truly understands, both intellectually and emotionally, that the abuse was not their fault, healing can truly begin. Personal blame and shame are no longer necessary.

Knowledge and intervention can play major parts in preventing childhood sexual abuse in future generations. There is much to learn from children's and family resource centers across the country and the communities they build. They understand that the nature of sexual abuse robs power from a person, and they strive to give back that power. They understand that many people do not report because they can easily be targeted, stigmatized, and re-traumatized throughout the process.

As with many topics, the childhood sexual abuse pendulum seems to sway in extreme measures, cycling from complete secrecy/taboo to awareness/action for prevention. This is an ongoing issue that calls for our constant attention.

One of the most important aspects to remember is compassion—for others and for yourself. Trauma is not necessarily defined by what happened; it is defined by your *perception of* what happened. Research shows that there can be long-term effects from trauma. Our bodies house traumas that can haunt us and torment us when we least expect them to. Until we are ready to reclaim the present, deal with the past, and know and feel the difference, we can get stuck. There is much information available on trauma-informed care, and it is our responsibility to learn about it and implement it in order to address the subject effectively.

Society has learned much from the Adverse Childhood Experiences (ACEs) study by the Center for Disease Control and Kaiser Permanente, which affirmed the fact that when a child is exposed to repeated doses of toxic stress, that stress will rewire their brain.[180]

When trauma does occur, I have come to understand that we pass trauma down unintentionally. Our bodies will lock on to trauma, and the trauma is communicated in a plethora of ways. It can torment us, and it waits until we are ready to deal with truth. Truth then rises, reclaiming reality.[181]

Denver's WINGS Foundation is in the process of conducting its One Voice Project. The One Voice Project is collaboration between a wide array of stakeholders, including survivors, loved ones, and providers from the sexual assault, domestic violence, health care, mental health and victims' services in Colorado. The project aims to measure access to care issues and opportunities for childhood sexual abuse survivors in order to strengthen the overall systems-wide response provided to them.[182]

Addressing childhood sexual abuse requires much energy and focus, leading to relief for survivors. Personally, I needed to get to know my four- and five-year-old self, teach her that she was not to blame, and explain that any shame was not hers.

Internal shame is not always about what happened but how it made you feel. Lori Gottlieb's statement in *Maybe You Should Talk to Someone* resonated with me: "There's no hierarchy of pain. Suffering shouldn't be ranked, because pain is not a contest."[183]

In other words, there is no intangible spectrum, and I acknowledge that the torment and shame I experienced from childhood sexual abuse was never mine to hold.

I find myself at forgiveness, self-compassion, and feeling

worthy of the internal growth that followed my lengthy, sometimes painful self-reflection. There are consequences that follow when acknowledging and digging deeper for internal growth. It is true that I have wavered on deep shame and release of shame, but I've learned that any forgiveness I need to give is to myself for torturing myself through beautiful autumn seasons and for not always being able to align my intellectual insights with emotional insights.

I still struggle sometimes, but the feelings of shame can go by the wayside forever. Perhaps my journey will bring hope, healing, and direction to other adult survivors of childhood sexual abuse, parents, and educators. We can all have a goal that education leads to future prevention.

I have attempted to communicate candidly while encouraging readers to look at their own lives openly as they begin to understand what sexual abuse is, how to identify it, and what they can do about it. I never thought of sharing my dark secret, and I certainly never considered writing a book about the subject of childhood sexual abuse.

What began as my personal healing path through therapy turned into a process of its own: *Meet Carey Jones*.

The University of Colorado School of Public Health research team, who worked on the One Voice Project, created this poem. It summarizes key themes from phase 1 of the project: Stigma and blame placed on the survivor. This poem also emphasizes the strength the research team saw when they talked to each survivor for this project.

## The Shame Is No Longer Mine

Authors: Yvonne Kellar-Guenther, Sarah Ballard, Kristin Banks, Jenell Brown, Maureen Dechico, Sydney Lawrence, Whit Oyler, Stacey Quesada, Grace Undis

I did not ask to grow here, in this
hard and unforgiving land;
A lone flower pushing up, but there is no helping hand.
I am often stepped on, overlooked
as others make their way;
Left alone to fight my demons each and every single day.
It is true that as a child I was sexually abused,
And now I stand before you while
you make excuses and accuse.
But I did nothing wrong, you see, I was young, just a pawn
Someone else with the power made the
rules, and I just had to go along.
I did not ask to grow here, that much is true,
But I survived despite the odds, and now what I ask of you
Is to know that while I hurt, the
blame does not lie with me.
I did nothing wrong, and I am ready to be free.

My ability to grow in this space reflects
the power I have to heal,
To exist beyond, be someone who has
grown past the whole ordeal.
Respect me and the strength I've
shown to share my story of
The childhood sexual abuse I endured
but was able to rise above.
I know that when you look, you see me
growing in the wrong place,
But look again, and you will see the beauty I create.

Dear reader,

Thank you for reading *Meet Carey Jones*. Childhood sexual abuse is a heavy subject that demands our attention. It is not a subject that people like to talk about, but it is necessary.

As a society, we can make an impact with our knowledge and actions. Awareness can help with prevention and with learning how to handle trauma effectively. I know that I would have benefitted from reading this book during recovery and healing.

As an author/speaker, I am available to speak about my personal process. If you would like to be in contact, please email me at info@meetcareyjones.com.

I wish you all the best.

Sincerely,
Christie Somes

## *Appendix 1*

# Organizations That Teach Prevention Programs for Adults and/or Children

Childhelp: www.childhelp.org

Colorado National Children's Alliance: www.colorado.nationalchildrensalliance.org

Darkness 2 Light: www.d2l.org

Mayo Clinic: www.mayoclinic.com

National Sexual Violence Resource Center: www.nsvrc.org

Parenting Safe Children: www.parentingsafechildren.com

RAINN: www.rainn.org

River Bridge Children's Resource Center: www.riverbridge.org

Stop It Now: www.stopitnow.org

WINGS Foundation: www.wingsfound.org

## *Appendix 2*

## Lorna Littner's List of Needs, Concerns, Learning Capabilities, Curiosities, and Behaviors

### Zero to Eighteen Months

- Bonding, touch intimacy begins.
- Quality of relationships is based on observation/interaction with other family members.
- Boys have penile erection (five to forty per day).
- Girls lubricate shortly after birth.
- They do not differentiate genitals from the rest of body (autoerotic).
- Gender-role conditioning begins.
- They start learning patterns of love, approval, and affection.

### Eighteen Months to Three Years

- They discover their own body parts and explore genitals and other parts of their bodies. Touching or rubbing genitals against a crib or toy feels good.

- They start to notice other bodies and comparing themselves to others.
- They show interest in different positions for urinating between boys and girls.
- They have little modesty.
- Gender-role conditioning continues.
- They begin to develop a foundation of self-worth and self-esteem.
- By the end of this stage, toilet training is usually completed.
- Attitudes about body image are beginning to form.

## Three to Six Years

- They begin to identify as boys or girls (as our culture defines it).
- They have increased interest in their bodies, masturbation, and self-pleasuring.
- They begin developing modesty while dressing or toileting.
- They begin developing social consciousness.
- Moral learning begins in a formal way.
- They begin identifying with their same-sex parent.
- They are curious about conception, pregnancy, and childbirth.
- They begin using sex words without understanding their meaning and play sex games with a childlike, nonerotic perspective.

## Seven to Twelve Years

- Social expectations become more important.
- They conform to the expectations of others (sexual stereotyping).
- There may be an emphasis on same-sex friends and experimentation.
- They are more concerned with fairness and rules.
- They develop self-esteem through accomplishments and positive relationships with adults.
- Sexual experimentation increases. They are curious about their bodies, which leads to looking at pictures, masturbation, crushes.
- They begin communicating formally with others about sex and sexuality (school, parents, religion).
- They exhibit concerns about the lack of physical changes associated with puberty.
- Girls begin to menstruate.

## Adolescence (Thirteen Plus)

- There is increased concern about physical appearance.
- Boys usually have first ejaculation in early part of this stage; one-quarter will experience this as a nocturnal emission (wet dream).
- There is uneven emotional growth, and impulse control varies.
- Peers become more important than family.
- They try many activities.
- Conflicts with parents lead to testing authority.
- They want more independence.

- They begin exploring partnered sexual intimacy (age of this varies with social and cultural norms)
- In the United States, more than half of girls have intercourse by seventeen and boys by sixteen and a half.
- They may need to make decisions about contraceptives, pregnancy, and/or parenting.
- They may begin experimenting with other "adult" behaviors like alcohol and drug use and relationships.
- They begin to develop their own value systems and plans for the future.

# Appendix 3

# A Developmental Profile by Dr. Gerald D. Alpern

Dr. Alpern's Developmental Profile
(www.wpspublish.com/DP3)

Determining at what level a child is functioning in the five essential developmental areas, from birth through pre-adolescence, offers parents, teachers, and other caregivers excellent information on how to best care for the child. Dr. Alpern's *Developmental Profile* is used to appropriately place children in school classes, therapy settings, as well as offer parents directions for furthering the child's skill levels at home. It can also be used to evaluate the benefits of any procedure for the child such as medicine, a course of therapy, or any educational program. This is done by testing the child at the start of any procedure, and, again, later when the procedure has had time to affect the targeted functioning. The evaluation report also serves to "diagnose" any developmental condition along with recommendations for further evaluations or formal treatments if warranted.

Parents, through a qualified clinician (e.g. teacher, physician or therapist) can easily find out their child's status in the five major developmental areas: Physical (strength, size, skills); Social-Emotional (psychological and cultural abilities); Cognitive (ability to learn and problem solve); Communication (use of expressive and receptive language); and Adaptive Behavior (ability to function at home, school, and community).

In about twenty minutes, parents simply answer what their child can and cannot do at the present time. They then receive an individualized report explaining where the child is developmentally (e.g., age equivalency scores) in each of the five areas along with individualized suggestions for helping the child progress in all five areas.

# Age-Appropriate Book Recommendations

There are numerous books to help with approaching the topic of sexual abuse in a nonthreatening, age-appropriate manner. Below is a list of some books we have found useful:

*My Body belongs to Me* by Jill Starishevsky and illustrated by Angela Padrón (ages 3–8)
Written as a poem, this book is written for young children to understand. This book helps explain boundaries to children in a nonthreatening, gentle manner. "Suggestions for Sharing This Book with Children" is filled with good advice for parents/educators.

*A Terrible Thing Happened* by Margaret M. Holmes and illustrated by Caru Pillo (Ages 4–8)
This story addresses children who have witnessed any type of trauma. It may also "give permission" to children to speak up if they have needs unknown to anybody else. "A Note to Parents and Caregivers" offers guidance and addresses the concept of secondary victims as "witnesses to a violent or traumatic event."

*My Body is Private* by Linda Walvoord Girard and illustrated by Rodney Pate
This candid book addresses healthy privacy and boundaries. In addition, an informative "A Note to Parents" written by Jon R. Conte, PhD, the University of Chicago, offers calming, helpful information, including the importance of open and honest communication with children.

*Please Tell! A Child's Story about Sexual Abuse* by Jessie
The author of this book is a child, Jessie, who powerfully discloses about her personal experience with sexual abuse. The book offers hope and gives permission to discuss the topic of sexual abuse, as well as information and guidance for children and adults. The foreword by Sandra Hewitt, PhD, is filled with helpful information for parents and caregivers.

*Some Secrets Should Never Be Kept* by Jayneen Sanders and illustrated by Craig Smith
The author of this book is a mother of three, a teacher, and an author who aims to give others an educational tool for teaching children about sexual abuse. The "Note to the Reader" gives specific suggestions for how to read/discuss this book with children as well as "General Body Safety Tips." The story is followed by discussion questions to create a comfortable means of communication between children and their caregivers.

*The Trouble with Secrets* by Karen Johnson and illustrated by Linda Johnson Forssell
This book addresses the important difference between secrets and surprises. Surprises are secrets that will eventually be told. Children should feel safe to tell secrets to adults who will help and protect them.

*I Can't Talk About It* by Doris Sanford and illustrated by Graci Evans
This book addresses the hidden emotions and fears of a sexually abused child who eventually finds the courage to disclose. Although having experienced painful feelings of being dirty, bad, hurt, sad, and guilty, she is able to have hope after disclosing to her mother.

*Some Parts Are Not for Sharing* by Julie K. Federico (6 Months and Up)
This book is written and illustrated to help convey important information to young children with ease. It is a great book to begin early conversation.

*It's Not the Stork!* by Robie H. Harris and illustrated by Michael Emberley
A book about girls, boys, babies, bodies, families, and friends.

*The Right Touch* by Sandy Kleven, LCSW, and illustrated by Jody Bergsma
As a way of teaching her little boy about sexual abuse, a mother tells him the story of a child who was lured into the neighbor's house to see some nonexistent kittens.

*A Secret Safe to Tell* by Naomi Hunter and illustrated by Karen Erasmus
This is a gentle book that encourages children to tell someone about any confusing feelings that they might be experiencing as a way of healing.

*The Impact of Pornography on Children, Youth, and Culture* by Cordelia Anderson
This booklet offers highlights of research related to the impact of pornography on children and youth. It also provides information and resources about what can be done to counter the harms of pornography and promote healthy sexual development.

*It's My Body* by Lory Freeman and illustrated by Carol Deach (Ages 2–8)
This classic book on personal safety teaches young children how to resist uncomfortable touch. The drawings are simple and expressive so that even the youngest reader can comprehend them. The text is simple and clear; positive, not scary.

*Protect Your Child from Sexual Abuse: A Parent's Guide* by Janie Hart-Rossi
A book to teach children how to resist uncomfortable touch.

*Who Has What?* by Robie H. Harris and illustrated by Nadine Bernard Westcott
On a day at the beach, siblings ask questions and figure out the similarities and differences between boys and girls in a humorous and honest way. With charming, informative

words and pictures, this book will reassure children that whether they have a girl's body or boy's body, their bodies are truly amazing—and wonderful!

*Uncle Willy's Tickles* by Marcie Aboff and illustrated by Kathleen Gartner
This book empowers children to speak up when they have a feeling or a thought.

*Who's the Boss of this Body?* by Meghan Hurley Backofen, LCSW and illustrated by FINAO Agency
This is an important book filled with valuable information to be shared with all children. Parents, educators, aunts, uncles, and grandparents—any adult who loves children will find this book to be a beneficial tool to begin ongoing necessary discussions with children about body safety. The book begins the process of normalizing discussion about *all* body parts by their correct name: an elbow, a fingernail, a penis, or a vagina. The book also greatly helps explain the difference between secrets and surprises and explains that it's never too late for a child to tell.

*How Much Is a Little Girl Worth?* by Rachael Denhollander and illustrated by Morgan Huff
Written by the author of *What Is A Girl Worth?*, this children's book is a child's poem of love and worthiness. The book is written to girls by a mother of three daughters. The author was the first gymnast to expose the atrocities of Larry Nassar inside USA Gymnastics. The author makes it clear that all young girls are made in the image of God.

# Bibliography

*Loving the Wounded Child Within*, R. Burney

*The Courage to Heal*, Ellen Bass and Laura Davis

*Miss America by Day*, Marilyn Van Derbur

*Survivors' and Loved Ones' Guide to Healing*, WINGS Foundation

*Mommy, Please Read This*, Troy Timmons

*The Sexual Healing Journey*, Wendy Maltz

*Surviving Childhood Sexual Abuse*, Carolyn Ainscough and Kay Toon

*Surviving Child Sexual Abuse*, Liz Hall and Siobhan Lloyd

*Trauma and Recovery*, Judith Herman

*The Traumatic Impact of Child Sexual Abuse: A Conceptualization*, David Finklehor and Angela Browne

*The Body Keeps the Score*, Dr. Bessel Van Der Kolk

*Helping Your Child Recover From Sexual Abuse*, Caren Adams and Jennifer Fay

*Parenting Safe Children*, Feather Berkower, LCSW

*Five Steps to Protecting Our Children*, Darkness to Light

*Be Fierce*, Gretchen Carlson

*Off Limits: A Parent's Guide to Keeping Kids Safe from Sexual Abuse*, Sandy Wurtele, PhD, and Feather Berkower, LCSW

# *Endnotes*

1. Black, Claudia. Unspoken Legacy. 2018. Central Recovery Press.
2. World Health Organization. 2006. ISPCAN. "Preventing child maltreatment: A guide to taking action and generating evidence." Geneva.
3. October 2017. Source: cnn.com
4. ucr.fbi.gov/recent-program-updates/reporting-rape-in-2013-revised
5. Van Derbur, Marilyn. 2012. *Miss America by Day*, Oak Hill Ridge Press.
6. Holy Bible, New Living Translation, 1996, 2004, 2015. Tyndale House Foundation.
7. Burney, R. *Loving the Wounded Child Within*. 1995. It is Joy to You and Me Enterprises, 31.
8. Burney, R. *Loving the Wounded Child Within*. 1995. It is Joy to You and Me Enterprises, 85.
9. Townsend, C. 2013. "Prevalence and consequences of child sexual abuse compared with other childhood experiences." Retrieved from www.d2l.org
10. Ibid.
11. Ibid.
12. Ibid.
13. WINGS Foundation. Retrieved from www. wingsfoun.org, Oct. 30, 2017.
14. Erin Merryn, 2017 www.erinmerryn.net.
15. Ibid.
16. RAINN. 2017. www.rainn.org
17. Darkness to Light. 2017. www.d2l.org. Statistics.

18  Ibid.
19  Ibid.
20  Van Derbur, Marilyn. 2012. *Miss America by Day*, Oak Hill Ridge Press.
21  Darkness to Light. 2017. www.d2l.org. Statistics.
22  Timmons, Troy. *Mommy, Please Read This*, 51-52.
23  Darkness to Light. 2017. www.d2l.org. Statistics.
24  Maltz, Wendy. 2012. *The Sexual Healing Journey*. HarperCollins, 38.
25  Townsend, C. 2013. "Prevalence and consequences of child sexual abuse compared with other childhood experiences." Retrieved from www.d2l.org.
26  Timmons, Troy. *Mommy, Please Read This*, 71-72.
27  Berkower, Feather. LCSW. Parenting Safe Children workshop.
28  Palumbo, Laura. 2017. National Violence Resource Center, www.nvrc.org.
29  Ibid.
30  Ibid.
31  Ibid.
32  Finkelhor, D. 1994. "Current information on the scope and nature of child sexual abuse." *The Future of Children*, vol. 4, no. 2, Sexual Abuse of Children, 31–53.
33  Putnam, F. 2003. "Ten-year research update review: Child sexual abuse." *Journal of the American Academy of Child and Adolescent Psychiatry*, 269–278.
34  Ibid.
35  Darkness to Light. 2017. www.d2l.org. Statistics.
36  Children's Bureau, U.S. Department of Health and Human Services. www.childwelfare.gov.
37  Darkness to Light. 2017. SignsofAbuse.pdf.
38  Darkness to Light. 2017. www.d2l.org.
39  Ibid.
40  Ibid.
41  Ibid.
42  Ibid.
43  Townsend, C. 2013. "Prevalence and consequences of child sexual abuse compared with other childhood experiences." Retrieved from www.d2l.org.
44  WINGS Foundation. 2017. www.wingsfound.org.

45  Darkness to Light. 2017. www.d2l.org.
46  Ibid.
47  Darkness to Light. 2017. www.d2l.org. Statistics.
48  Ascent Children's Health Services. www.ascentchs.com/mental-health/child-abuse/symptoms-signs-effects.
49  Ibid.
50  Ainscough, C and Toon, K. 2000. *Surviving Childhood Sexual Abuse.* Da Capo Press, 49.
51  Black, Claudia. *Unspoken Legacy.* 2018. Central Recovery Press.
52  Hall, M. and Hall, J. 2011. "The long-term effects of childhood sexual abuse: Counseling implications." Retrieved from counselingoutfitters.com/vistas/vistas11/Article_19.pdf.
53  WINGS. 2014. *Survivors' and Loved Ones' Guide to Healing*, 137.
54  Elements Behavorial Health. 2010. www.elementsbehavioralhealth.com/trauma-ptsd/anger-and-trauma/.
55  WINGS. 2014. *Survivors' and Loved Ones' Guide to Healing*, 133.
56  WINGS. 2014. *Survivors' and Loved Ones' Guide to Healing*, 134.
57  WINGS. 2014. *Survivors' and Loved Ones' Guide to Healing*, 138.
58  Darkness to Light. 2017. www.d2l.org.
59  WINGS. 2014. *Survivors' and Loved Ones' Guide to Healing*, 135.
60  Ibid.
61  Ibid.
62  Ainscough, C. and Toon, K. 2000. *Surviving Childhood Sexual Abuse.* Da Capo Press.
63  Ascent Children's Health Services. www.ascentchs.com/mental-health/childabuse/ symptoms-abuse/symptoms-signs-effects.
64  WINGS. 2014. *Survivors' and Loved Ones' Guide to Healing*, 132–133.
65  Hall, M., and Hall, J. 2011. The long-term effects of childhood sexual abuse: Counseling implications. Retrieved from: counselingoutfitters.com/vistas/vistas11/Article_19.pdf.
66  WINGS. 2014. *Survivors' and Loved Ones' Guide to Healing*, 114.
67  Bass, E. and Davis, L. 2008. *The Courage to Heal*, HarperCollins, 13.
68  WINGS. 2014. *Survivors' and Loved Ones' Guide to Healing*, 115.
69  Ibid.
70  Ibid.
71  Bass, E. and Davis, L. 2008. *The Courage to Heal*, HarperCollins, 16.

72 Turner S, Mota N, Bolton J, Sareen J. 2018. "Self-medication with alcohol or drugs for mood and anxiety disorders: A narrative review of the epidemiological literature." www.ncbi.nlm.nih.gov/pubmed/29999576.
73 WINGS. 2014. *Survivors' and Loved Ones' Guide to Healing*, 54.
74 Ibid.
75 Eating Disorder Hope 2017. www.eatingdisorderhope.com.
76 Ibid.
77 Ibid.
78 Darkness to Light. 2017. www.d2l.org
79 Bass, E. and Davis, L. 2008. *The Courage to Heal,* HarperCollins, 25.
80 Ainscough, C. and Toon, K. 2000. *Surviving Childhood Sexual Abuse*, Da Capo Press, 139.
81 WINGS. 2014. *Survivors' and Loved Ones' Guide to Healing*, 129.
82 Ibid.
83 WINGS. 2014. *Survivors' and Loved Ones' Guide to Healing*, 267.
84 Ibid.
85 Ibid.
86 American Psychological Association. 2017. www.apa.org/topics/trauma.
87 Ibid.
88 Ibid.
89 Ibid.
90 Maltz, W. 1991. *The Sexual Healing Journey*, 44.
91 Herman, J. 1992. *Trauma and Recovery*, 96.
92 Herman, J. 1992. *Trauma and Recovery*, 28.
93 Herman, J. 1992. *Trauma and Recovery*, 32.
94 Mayo Clinic. 2017. www.mayoclinic.org.
95 WINGS. 2014. *Survivors' and Loved Ones' Guide to Healing*, 137.
96 Finkelhor, D. and Browne, A. 1985. *The Traumatic Impact of Child Sexual Abuse: A Conceptualization*.
97 Ibid.
98 Ibid.
99 Ibid.
100 WINGS. 2014. *Survivors' and Loved Ones' Guide to Healing*, 144–145.
101 Finkelhor, D. and Browne, A. 1985. *The Traumatic Impact of Child Sexual Abuse: A Conceptualization*.

102  Ibid.
103  Ibid.
104  Herman, J. 1992. *Trauma and Recovery*, 113.
105  Van Der Kolk, Dr. B. 2014. *The Body Keeps the Score*. Penguin, 21.
106  Ibid.
107  Novick, Dr. D. (2018) New Policies Integrate Care for Traumatized Children.
108  Ibid.
109  Ibid.
110  Ibid.
111  Darkness to Light. 2017. www.d2l.org
112  Ibid.
113  Townsend, C. 2013. "Prevalence and consequences of child sexual abuse compared with other childhood experiences." Charleston, S.C., Darkness to Light. Retrieved from www.D2L.org.
114  Ibid.
115  Van Derbur, M. 2012. *Miss America by Day*. Oak Hill Ridge Press.
116  Townsend, C. 2013. "Prevalence and consequences of child sexual abuse compared with other childhood experiences." Charleston, SC, Darkness to Light. Retrieved from www.D2L.org.
117  Ibid.
118  Ibid.
119  Ibid.
120  Ibid.
121  Ibid.
122  Ibid.
123  Ibid.
124  Ibid.
125  Ibid.
126  Bass, E. and Davis, L. 2008. *The Courage to Heal,* HarperCollins, 106.
127  Townsend, C. 2013. "Prevalence and consequences of child sexual abuse compared with other childhood experiences." Charleston, SC, Darkness to Light. Retrieved from www.D2L.org.
128  www.mediacollege.com/journalism/interviews/leading-questions.html (2) Ceci, 1994; Ceci and Bruck, 1993a, 1993b; Ceci, Loftus, Leichtman, and Bruck, 1994; Leichtman and Ceci, in press; Clarke-Stewart, Thompson, and Lepore, 1989; Haugaard and

Alhusen, 1992; Thompson, Clarke-Stewart, Meyer, Pathak, and Lepore, 1991.
129 Ibid.
130 WINGS. 2014 *Survivors' and Loved Ones' Guide to Healing*, 121.
131 River Bridge Regional Center. 2017. www.riverbridge.org.
132 WINGS. 2014. *Survivors' and Loved Ones' Guide to Healing*, 121.
133 Ibid.
134 Curran, L. 2009. *Trauma Competency: A Clinician's Guide*. PESI.
135 WINGS. 2014. *Survivors' and Loved Ones' Guide to Healing* 122–123.
136 www.goodtherapy.org/blog/psychpedia/trigger).
137 Rorer; *Journal of Rational-Emotive and Cognitive-Behavior Therapy*, December 1999, volume 17, issue 4, 217–236.
138 N., Pam MS, "EMOTIONAL INSIGHT 1," in PsychologyDictionary.org, April 7, 2013, www.psychologydictionary.org/emotional-insight-1/ (accessed August 16, 2019).
139 U.S. Department of Veterans Affairs. (2017) PTSD: National Center for PTSD. Anniversary Reactions. www.ptsd.va.gov/professional/treat/essentials/anniversary reactions.asp.
140 Van Der Kolk, Dr. B. 2014. *The Body Keeps the Score*. Penguin, 178.
141 Van Der Kolk, Dr. B. 2014. *The Body Keeps the Score*. Penguin, 267.
142 Van Der Kolk, Dr. B. 2014. *The Body Keeps the Score*. Penguin, 268.
143 Van Der Kolk, Dr. B. 2014. *The Body Keeps the Score*. Penguin, 2.
144 Van Der Kolk, Dr. B. 2014. *The Body Keeps the Score*. Penguin, 275.
145 WINGS Foundation. 2017. www.wingsfound.org.
146 WINGS. 2014. *Survivors' and Loved Ones' Guide to Healing*, 199.
147 Michael, R. 2018, "What Self-Care Is and What It Isn't," psychcentral.com/blog/what-self-care-is-and-what-it-isnt-2/.
148 Ibid.
149 WINGS. 2014. *Survivors' and Loved Ones' Guide to Healing*, 252.
150 Ibid.
151 Ibid.
152 Ibid.
153 WINGS. 2014. *Survivors' and Loved Ones' Guide to Healing*, 253.
154 www.allpsychologyschools.com/psychology/psychology-vs-psychiatry/.
155 www.talkspace.com/blog/therapist-psychotherapist-complete-definition/.

156 G. Carlson. *Be Fierce*. 1997. Hachette Book Group.
157 Berkower, F.; "Parenting Safe Children," (April 2018) Workshop/ Carbondale, Colorado.
158 Wurtele, Sandy and Berkower, Feather. *Off Limits: A Parent's Guide to Keeping Kids Safe from Sexual Abuse*. 2010. The Safer Society Press.
159 Darkness to Light, 2017. www.d2l.org.
160 Ibid.
161 Ibid.
162 Ibid.
163 Ibid.
164 Ibid.
165 Darkness to Light, 2017. The 5 Steps To Protecting Our Children; www.d2l.org.
166 Darkness to Light. 2017. www.d2l.org.
167 Adams, C. and Fay, J. 1998. *Helping Your Child Recover From Sexual Abuse*. University of Washington Press.
168 Ibid.
169 Ibid.
170 Ibid.
171 Ibid.
172 Darkness to Light. 2017. www.d2l.org
173 Ibid.
174 Athens County Child Advocacy Center; 2017. "A handbook for caregivers of sexually abused children," www.athenscac.org.
175 Childhood sexual abuse hotline. 2017. www.childhelp.org.
176 Darkness to Light, 2017. www.d2l.org.
177 Ibid.
178 Ibid.
179 Ibid.
180 ACEs. www.cdc.gov/violenceprevention/childabuseandneglect/acestudy/index.html. retrieved 9.20.19.
181 Ibid.
182 One Voice Project. WINGS Foundation. 2019. www.wingsfound.org.
183 Gottlieb, Lori. *Maybe You Should Talk to Someone*. 2019. Houghton Mifflin Harcourt, 294.

# *About the Authors*

## Christie Somes

Christie Somes is a survivor of childhood sexual assaults that happened when she was just four and five years old. She carried many of the effects of her abuse for decades, not understanding the debilitating emotional, mental, and physical tolls the abuse created. In order to confront these effects, she has gone through a twelve-year journey of therapy and group support to bring about understanding, learning, and healing. Her personal knowledge of the subject of childhood sexual abuse and the practical information she learned through the healing process forms the basis for *Meet Carey Jones*.

Christie Somes is a wife, mother of three adult children, grandmother, daughter, sister, and friend. She is an entrepreneur, certified yoga instructor, and avid hiker. As a lover of the outdoors, she can also be found snowshoeing and horseback riding. Christie lives with her husband on their ranch in Colorado, and above all else, she enjoys spending time with family and friends.

# Gerald D. Alpern, Ph.D.

Dr. Alpern is a former full professor at Indiana University Medical School and a clinical and developmental psychologist. His "Developmental Profile" series (wpspublish.com/DP3), which evaluates children's development, has been used throughout many countries for more than thirty years. His clinical practice of more than fifty years involved working with children, families, and individuals. His writings include publications for both professionals and the lay public. His last book, *Vets for Vets,* is based on his hands-on work with the traumas of returning veterans. His contributions to the present book reflect his extensive clinical experience dealing with childhood traumas.

# Other Bios

## Lorna Littner, LMSW

Lorna Littner, MS, LMSW, is a human sexuality educator who teaches to a wide range of students, including children in grades K–12, young adults in colleges and universities, and paraprofessional and professional staff in a range of family and child service agencies. Currently, she is focused on staff training and development. Her areas of special interest include child sexual abuse and the provision of quality sexuality education to students with cognitive disabilities, including those on the autism spectrum.

# Feather Berkower, LCSW

Feather Berkower, LCSW, is a one of the nation's leading experts in child sexual assault prevention. She is the coauthor of *Off Limits: A Parent's Guide to Keeping Kids Safe from Sexual Abuse* and the founder of the child sexual abuse prevention workshop Parenting Safe Children. She has dedicated her career, which now spans more than three decades, to educating parents and youth professionals on how to make their communities off-limits to child sexual assault. Using her community-based approach, she has trained more than one hundred thousand schoolchildren, parents, and youth professionals across the United States.